Inkslinger 2

inkslinger

2

Planning Your Amazing Book

Finnian Burnett
and
Kimberly Cooper Griffin

NiGHT
RiVeR
PRESS

Night River Press
880 South Saint Paul Street
Denver CO 80209
skeetieb@me.com www.nightriverpress.com

Ordering Information:
Quantity sales. Special discounts are available on quantity purchases by corporations, associations, and others. For details, contact the publisher at the address above.

Printed in the United States of America
Paperback Cover: ISBN 978-0-9964349-9-7
Ebook: ISBN 979-8-9852528-0-4

Library of Congress Control Number: 2021922782

Editor: Marlo Garnsworthy
Cover Designer & Graphics: Shelle Pourmanafzadehardabili

Acknowledgements

Finnian Burnett: This book couldn't have happened without the constant encouragement of my writing partner, Kimberly Cooper Griffin. The hours we spent on Zoom either discussing the work or researching subjects was an invaluable part of this process. Of course, I also acknowledge the importance of our video writing dates where I'd pause in my writing to get on Facebook and look up to see her glowering face standing as a stern warning to shut off social media and get back to work.

I also want to give a shout out to my dear friend, author Tammy Bird who is always available for a discussion about the importance of the Oxford comma or whether an in-text citation should contain a page number.

I'd like to thank Lord Gordo for bring a constant peaceful furry presence on my desk.

Finally, I want to thank my lovely wife, August Van Stralen. Being married to another writer means she never gets tired of conversations about writing, she loves to jump on a search engine with me to look up obscure craft rules, and she somehow always manages to help me get unstuck when I'm at an impasse, in writing or in life.

❖

Kimberly Cooper Griffin: Thank you so much for agreeing to write this with me, Finn. You are a constant source of inspiration for me through things like writing dates and thoughtful feedback on my work, but also in the dedication you have to your writing, your continuing efforts to learn, but, most importantly, you just being you. You're a font of joy and wisdom, and you can stop shaking your head—you are.

I also appreciate my teammates at Inkstacks who have made it possible for me to accomplish my dreams of helping other writers get their stories written. Without them, I would still be managing software development during the days and scribbling my stories during the nights.

And, as always, I couldn't have done any of this without the support of my wonderful family, friends, and readers. Thank you all from the bottom of my writerly heart.

Table of Contents

Introduction

Hello, Dear Writer.

In our first book, *Inkslinger—99-Day Guided Writing Experience*, we gave you a guided path for writing a book by providing the information needed to successfully plan and compose a solid manuscript. We also devised a 99-day plan in which to write it. And finally, we told you how to rewrite and revise to turn the ugly first draft into a smooth manuscript that will be ready to send to a professional editor or to pitch to an agent.

In this book, *Inkslinger 2—Planning Your Amazing Book*, we take the planning topics we summarized in *Inkslinger—99-Day Guided Writing Experience* and expand on them. We dive deeper into the plotting and preparation required to craft a truly excellent book. We try not to put you to sleep with history or the boring details you get in classes; we provide practical knowledge to give you the confidence to write the book you've been wanting to write. We teach you how to plan your book so that when you sit down to write it, you know exactly what you need to do to craft your story.

We are very aware that some writers prefer not to plot or prepare—they're daredevil word acrobats, preferring to dive right into the thick of things, throwing out words all willy-nilly, acting like elephants on unicycles charging through the room, brandishing flaming swords, scared of nothing. We're not saying that isn't a reasonable way to write. Not at all. If that's you, you go, you! Be that badass writer! We'll be over here with the fire extinguishers, unguent, and bandages if you need us. However, if you want a tight plot with consistent characters and a deep, rich setting, we will argue that planning is key.

That's where we come in. This deeper dive into the planning elements necessary to craft your book is meant to give you a solid foundation on which to start. We'll walk you through target audience, plotting, character sketches, setting— basically everything you need to write your book. With these tools in place before you start, you'll be well equipped to craft a successful novel.

How this amazing book works

This is a multi-media book. (What the heck does that mean, Kimberly and Finnian?) That means you not only get to read this book, but you can also click on the links scattered throughout to watch videos of the authors discussing each subject. You'll hear their personal experiences of using these craft elements, and they'll do an even deeper exploration of the topics—often in snazzy ties and smart-looking glasses, sipping coffee that gets cold because we have to do retake after retake when one of us breaks out into hysterical laughter. Because writing is fun, and talking about writing is even funner. (Funner *is* a word. Fight us!)

Additionally, we give you exercises to try yourself, resources to dig more deeply into the subjects, and examples, and we supply you with worksheets, one for each topic we cover. Who doesn't love worksheets? They're meant to help you focus your creativity and organize your book. They take you through your journey from the first spark of inspiration to the glorious first sentence of your novel, "Once upon a time..." and keep you going because you'll have planned out all the steps from the start.

Do you have to use this book in the order the topics are presented? No. We organized this book in what, to us, seems a logical order for writing a novel. But you can skip around if you like. You may have an incredible character in mind, and you're not exactly sure what kind of plot you're going to give them, so sketch that character out first. That may even help you work out your plot. Conversely, you may have only the inkling of a character in mind and, as you start outlining the plot, the character may develop as additional details of the plot come to you.

Because we're writers ourselves, we know that writers are creatives, and creatives are unpredictable creatures. You can't constrain us. We do what we want. So, seriously, go ahead and skip around. Pick and choose what you want to work on. It all works together, no matter what sequence you go in.

In fact, we did it ourselves. We skipped around when we were working out the character, plot, and setting for *The Shadow Hunters*, the example story you'll see us develop in this book. As interesting aspects of the characters developed, and as we discussed the plot, we went back and forth on character sketches and plot outlining. Sometimes, we'd start working on a character and realize they needed more of an arc, which sent us back to the outline. In other words, we had several moments of chasing something shiny before settling back into the discipline of work. Ultimately, we had a solid plan for *The Shadow Hunters*, and you can look forward to seeing it actually get published. It's basically proof that the planning we teach you in this book works.

In *Inkslinger—99 Day Guided Writing Experience*, we gave you the framework to use when writing your book. We walked you through the basic technical skills you need to craft a story. In this book, our aim is to help you give your readers a richer experience by developing those basic skills even further. Therefore, in *Inkslinger 2—Planning Your Amazing Book*, we will go more in-depth into planning the following topics:

Target Audience—What readers do you want to reach, and how do you make sure you give them what they want?

Genre—Genre often dictates the style and content of a story, so you'll want to be clear about your genre to ensure you give your readers what they expect, as well as use the right tools for telling the story.

Plot and Outlining—Whether you're a detailed planner or a seat of your pants writer, a tight plot is the best way to tell a story. Creating an outline, either a simple one with bullet points, or one in great detail, will not only save you from rambling, but it will keep you moving forward and help prevent you from getting into writing dead ends.

Point of View—Who or what is the best narrator for your story? Point of view can give your reader a close-up look into the characters or action in your story, or it can add a sense of mystery by standing back and observing in a more clinical fashion. Picking the best point of view for your story can dramatically affect how the story is told.

Setting—The environment in which your characters and story exist plays a pivotal role in developing the right tone for your story.

Character Sketches—A complex and multi-faceted character is a way to get your reader invested in your story, and knowing your character before you start writing them will make them more authentic and believable.

Our job is to give you a guided path for creating your book. Your job is to show up with your ideas, organize them into a workable plan, and just write.

You can watch a video of Finnian and Kimberly talking about the making of this book if you go to YouTube at: https://youtu.be/H-gTQr-A7VM.

So, let's get going, shall we?

Target Audience

Target Audience—A specific group of people your work is written for, with the intended purpose of appealing to, amusing, persuading, helping, educating, entertaining, or allowing escape.

I never think in terms of target audience. I try to write what makes me laugh, so I'm the target audience. I guess I just hope there's another person in America like me. - **Eric Idle**

Introduction

Before we get into this Super Important chapter on target audiences, we should probably answer a question you may already have. What is a target audience other than the basic definition we already gave?

A target audience is a marketing term used to describe the best customer for a product. To an author, it is the best reader for their book. You could look at a target audience as the group of people who are most likely to buy your book, but it goes beyond that. It also describes the people who *need* your book. A target audience has a need they want to satisfy, and you have a book that satisfies that need. That intersection is the sweet spot. If you can define that set of people, you will build a loyal fan base for your book.

Now, to answer the second question that probably emerged as you read the above: Is it important for you to care about target audiences?

We say yes.

We get it, though. It's not always sexy, but it *is* important to make sure you not only know who your target audience is, but you also know how to sell to them. After all, you're writing your book with the intention that someday someone will read it. You may think this is the publisher's job, or you might believe your book is going to appeal to one hundred percent of the population. But neither of those ideas is true, and we'll explain why in the next section.

In the meantime, no one is going to force you to understand your target audience. In fact, you can flat out ignore the entire concept and still write incredibly breathtaking books that capture the hearts and fancies of people ages nine to ninety-nine. It's possible. And some writers prefer to ignore things like marketing plans when they start writing their book. After all, who wants all those ugly details weighing down their creativity? No one.

But there are good reasons to at least understand what a target audience is and how it can be a pretty powerful tool if you take the time to determine who that audience is. Stick with us to find out why.

What It's All About

Still here?

Yes! Let's talk about target audience!

Starting simply, people are naturally curious about writers. You can't blame them, can you? Writers *are* a fascinating breed. Get used to the questions. You'll be asked a lot of them. The first question people invariably ask is, "What kind of books do you write?" What they're actually asking is whether your story is something they might be interested in reading. While you're still in the massively creative stage of the process, it's okay if you don't know the specific answer to that question. People will forgive you for fumbling through the description of what your book is about while you're still writing it.

But eventually, you'll want to have a concise answer for them. Wouldn't it feel good to rattle off a sentence that conveys exactly what the book is about while telling them who the book is for? Having an answer like that will keep them interested in talking to you about it, and you'll get to talk about your favorite thing.

Who knows? It might even help you with the story itself. You want to compose the best story you can, right? You want to include the details that will resonate with your readers. Many books with intriguing plots have failed because the writer did something minor, such as using vocabulary outside of their readers' interest. Don't let this happen to you. Knowing your target audience will help prevent you from making that kind of mistake.

While you're mulling that over, also know this. As you get close to the end of your book, you will have to decide what to do when you're finished. Planning now can make that decision feel a lot less overwhelming.

Maybe your dream is to sell it to an agent or a publisher. There's a lot of appeal in working with people who know all the details of the publishing business and have the experience to back it up. It saves you from having to learn it all yourself.

However, before you get too excited about the very attractive idea of just handing your manuscript over to an agent or a publisher to deal with things like defining your target audience, it's a good time to tell you that it doesn't work exactly like that. At some point, you'll have to pitch the book to them, and a big part of that pitch is defining your target audience. First, they need to know if your book fits the profile of the books they publish. Second, they'll want to know why your book will make them more money than the thousands of other books being pitched to them. And third, they'll want to know if they're dealing with a person who takes writing and selling books seriously, the kind of person who believes in their work and who will do extra to make sure their book gets the visibility it needs to stand out from all the other books being pitched to them. Because of the above-mentioned reasons, most submission processes require a marketing plan with your book proposal. Because, like it or not, you *are* your brand, which we will discuss a little later in this chapter, and part of selling a book is selling yourself.

Now, let's say you're not going to pitch to anyone. You're going to self-publish. There's a huge appeal to being in charge of your own writing and publishing journey. Number one, you don't have to play by anyone else's rules. Who cares if you don't know how to do it yet? There is an enormous amount of information and no-cost education about each and every step of the writing and publishing process on the Internet, so you can learn it yourself. You are the boss of your writing and publishing process.

Truth Bomb: You'll still want to know who your target audience is because you'll be the one promoting and marketing your book. And as great as your book is, most people don't buy a book with the *hope* they will like it. They want to know it's a book they'll at least *probably* like. If you self-publish, you'll need a marketing plan. Knowing your target audience is key to writing an effective blurb, the short summary of the book that goes on the back or the inside cover of the book. Also, you'll need to promote your book through advertising and author events, where you'll be asked over and over again what your book is about and who it will appeal to.

See where we're going with this? We want you to be prepared for all these questions.

If that's not enough to convince you, here are some other reasons you need to understand your target audience:

- To establish your brand

- To craft your story

- To know how to allocate your marketing/promotional budget

- To establish the right tone, POV (point of view), language, world-building, story beats, etc., for your genre

- To build an effective pitch of your work to an agent, publisher, best friend, family members, and most importantly, readers

- To ensure the information you want to convey is delivered to the right readers

- To avoid getting frustrated when people don't understand what you're trying to say about your current project

- To choose the right cover art

- To reach the most lucrative market for your work (We know you want to write for the art of it, but there's also the money, let's be real.)

Suffice it to say, a huge part of any marketing plan is an intimate knowledge of your target audience and what you want to become of your hard work.

How do you define your target audience?

To some, it may feel like it's just some big, nebulous concept that people pretend to understand but really don't—at least at the level they need to craft a successful marketing plan.

It helps to think about your target audience in simple

terms—as the type of person who would want to read your book. A lot of factors go into who that type of person is, but defining this is the first step. Once you have that theoretical person in mind, you'll figure out the individual factors that set them apart from other readers. There are several ways to determine the factors before you even start writing, which we'll get into a little bit later, but in the meantime, not only will defining your perfect reader help you sell your book, but it will help you craft the story more specifically to delight the readers you wish to reach—if you know who they are early enough in the process.

One of the most common ways writers go wrong during the important exercise of defining the target audience is having a desire for their story to appeal to everyone. Let's face it, most writers would love to be the next best-selling author. All of us say it's all about releasing the story inside us, but there's always that private dream that our book will resonate with all the people, that our writing is so universally compelling that everyone on Earth will want to read it.

We're here to tell you it's amazing when a book does break the barriers of market segments and specific audiences, but when it does, it's not because the author has written a phenomenal book—even if the book is phenomenal. It's because they knew who they were writing for and did it exceptionally well.

> *I can't tell you the key to success, but the key to failure is trying to please everyone.*—**Ed Sheeran**

To be even more specific, the best way to write a boring book is by trying to please all readers.

The better way to appeal to a larger audience is to write

something specific very well, thus attracting readers who might not be naturally drawn to it, but who might be pulled in and introduced to it through the enthusiasm of the target audience. Ever wonder why people want to have their book picked up by a celebrity's book club? This is the reason. Get your book about the crafting of 18TH century nails into Oprah's hands, and watch your audience explode!

If you're writing your first book, or it's the first time you're writing a particular kind of book, you will need to make assumptions based on looking at comparable titles. If this isn't your first book of this type, you can use actual data from your previous sales to define your target audience. But before you look at comparable titles and start analyzing your previous sales information, you want to really understand your brand.

So, let's talk about your brand.

What is an author's brand? It is the identity that distinguishes them as unique among the totality of all authors. It's made up of a number of aspects. For example:

- the genre

- a distinct voice

- a type of audience

- a style of cover

- the author's individual personality

- a social media presence

And probably others. Regardless of the specific aspects, the amalgam of them defines the author's brand, and it is the basis on how an author markets themselves to the people who will like their work.

Sometimes, an author may already possess a unique image just by being themselves and writing what they want to write. Their persona is who they really are. They are aware of how they are perceived by their readers, and their work and image are consistent with what appeals to them. This would be their brand. For example, Stephen King comes to mind. He enjoys horror books, and he writes them. He tends to dress in black, and his interests align with his work. He's even put out a coffee table book about gargoyles called *Nightmares in the Sky*.

And sometimes, the author specifically nurtures their brand in a deliberate attempt to appeal to a certain audience. They might do this by creating a pen name that suits a certain genre or dressing in a way that brings to mind the kinds of books they write. For instance, Louis L'Amour, the prolific and popular author of rough and tough American Western novels, grew up around cowboys and livestock and even wore bolo ties and Western clothing, but he initially wrote under the pen name Tex Burns because he didn't believe his real name sounded like a writer of Western novels.

Further, when it comes to finding a publisher, having a brand is a bonus. Even if you're trying to sell your first book, being able to say, "And I'm following my first military cover-up thriller with a second military cover-up thriller," shows that you are already looking to build a career for yourself writing in that genre. Demonstrating to a publisher that you've established your brand or that you're in the process of establishing it lends weight to your query.

If you haven't already established your brand, the following will help you learn how. First, let's answer these questions:

- What kind of story, or genre, are you writing? (Genres often come with specific audiences already identified.)

- Why are you writing this particular story?

- What message do you want your story to impart?

- Which general audience will the message or theme best suit?

Answering the above questions will allow you to dive into the deeper questions you'll need to ask to really understand your brand and identify the best audience for your book.

Now, think about your ideal reader. Do you write the books you like to read? That's easy. Describe yourself. You're probably a good model for your target audience. Be specific. Maybe you aren't the ideal, or typical, reader for your book. Perhaps you're a twenty-four-year-old male who works as a roughneck and you also write historical romance novels. Eighty-four percent of romance novel readers are female, usually between the ages of thirty and fifty-four. You are not your target audience. You might need to do some research or take some educated guesses and try to sketch out who you think the ideal reader is.

Try to define the following characteristics of your Ideal Reader:

- Demographics
  - Age
  - Geography
  - Gender
  - Income level
  - Education level
  - Marital or family status
  - Occupation
  - Cultural or ethnic background
- Individual Personal Details
  - Personality
  - Attitudes
  - Values
  - Interests/hobbies
  - Lifestyle
  - Behavior

- Digging Deeper

  - What sets my target audience apart from others?

  - Does my target audience specifically like/dislike certain things?

  - Is there certain content that is more or less appropriate for my audience?

  - What tone/voice/language is appropriate for my target audience?

As we noted before, another easy way to define your ideal reader is to describe the readers of comparable titles, also known by the cool kids in the industry as comp titles. Comp titles are books close enough to yours that you will probably have common readers. If you write supernatural fiction, you may find comp titles by Stephen King, Dean Koontz, and Clive Barker, all of whom write horror and supernatural fiction.

When you pitch your book, the publisher will ask about comp titles if you haven't already mentioned them, so it's a good idea to have examples prepared. Earlier, we told you that the best way to please no one is to try to please everyone. Publishers like to ask about comp titles because they are a good way to narrow focus so you can concentrate on writing for people who will absolutely love your work. These are your target audience because they will be loyal readers and become one of your best sales tools through word of mouth and, if you're lucky, by writing rave reviews about your books.

Ways to identify comp titles:

1. Follow your comp authors on social media.

2. Join groups targeted to fans of your comp authors.

3. Ask people if they'd be willing to take a survey designed to gather information about your target audience.

4. Think about your secondary audience. If your primary audience consists of Stephen King fans who love stand-alone monster stories, but you also have elements of gothic horror, remember to consider fans of that material, as well.

5. Use social media analytics. If you're serious about writing, you should consider starting at least one social media page specific to your writing and posting content relevant to your work and which aligns with your brand. (This might also help you start building your target audience.)

Once you've found a few good comparable examples, do some analysis. Try to get into the minds of your audience. Who are they? What do they like? What do they dislike? What are some of their behaviors? Do a deep dive into who these people are. This kind of analysis will help you determine key aspects of your target audience.

Summary

We've given you a ton of information about understanding

and defining your target audience. You now know what a target audience is and how to identify *your* target audience. Along the way, we also told you about using comp titles to help you do some of this and about the importance of developing your brand. Because of this knowledge, you have the tools to reach the people who will most enjoy your work and delight them by giving them what they want—which will also result in them telling others about your work so you can increase your fan base.

We'll let you in on a secret: we know this isn't the sexiest skill you need to master as a writer—at least, we *hope* this isn't the sexist thing. (If it is, we're very sorry. Sorry for what, exactly? We actually don't know, but we *are* sorry.) However, it *is* important. At the very least, knowing who you're writing for will give you clarity and focus in your writing. In addition, it will help you tailor your work in such a way as to give your audience just what they want, even if they aren't sure what that is themselves. And, finally, it gives you the knowledge you need to build your audience so you can get your work into the hands of the most people you can. There's a lot of power in this.

If you got this far, we think you'll do well at this writer thing. The remaining chapters should be informative and maybe even a little entertaining.

Admit it. You're hooked!

Frequently asked questions

What are the basic reasons for understanding target audience?

Almost everything you do when writing a book should be performed with your target audience in mind. It helps you make decisions about genre, characters, point of view, tone, story line, word choice, cover style, length of story... We could go on and on.

What do you do if you haven't picked out your target audience before you start writing your story?

You can start by making yourself the target audience and write what you would like to write. Many writers do this by default. There is truth to the common advice to write what you know.

Does defining a target audience apply to both fiction and nonfiction work?

Absolutely. It applies to both fiction and nonfiction for the same reasons. An author needs to understand who they're writing for to successfully provide the content the specific audience wants, needs, or expects. There is nothing worse than for someone to sit down to read something and find out it isn't what they were expecting.

If it helps, imagine a reader purchasing a book called *How to Pick Out the Best Horse*, expecting to become more knowledgeable about a future purchase of a real live horse for their stable, only to open the book to find it's a book about pummel horses, sawhorses, or even seahorses. The simplest exercise in defining the target audience would have told the writer the title, book cover, and blurb displayed on the book cover should have been more specific.

I write in multiple genres. Am I out of luck in defining a brand, let alone a target audience?

Absolutely not! In fact, you can approach your target audience in a couple of ways. One way is to cultivate your audience for each genre. In other words, follow all the advice in this chapter for each genre in which you write.

Another way is to simply cultivate a target audience of people who like to read across genres and who will absolutely adore the fact that they can follow one author and still satisfy their taste for change. Think historical fiction. This wasn't a thing until the early 19TH century when authors such as Sir Walter Scott and Honoré de Balzac began to use it in their novels. Just know that it's a risk to do something that has not been done before. You may end up reaching fewer readers if you try something people have a hard time accepting. But, hey, you just learned how to identify your target audience and develop your brand. That's how innovation starts, finding a need in a target audience and satisfying it.

Recommended Resources

https://www.writersdigest.com/publishing-faqs/does-your-target-audience-exist-use-this-simple-trick-to-figure-it-out

Discussion Time

Finnian and Kimberly talk about why defining a target audience is important to them.

Target Audience: https://youtu.be/czjpQToF6fw

Try it out

Getting your feet wet:

Identify your brand and target audience by using the information you learned in this chapter.

Diving right in:

If you have already established a brand for your kind of writing, write a paragraph or two about what that brand is and, using the information you learned in this chapter, identify a few ways to get the attention of readers for your last book or a book you are currently working on. Focus specifically on the audience you want to reach.

Genre

Genre – This is the category in which your work falls, determined by the variety of qualities of the work shares with other works in the same category.

I also love the zombie genre, my zombie fandom going way back to 'Night of the Living Dead.' And 'The Walking Dead' is truly the ultimate representation of that sensibility in the comic book genre.—**Gale Anne Hurd**

Introduction

What kind of books do you write?

This is probably the first question a person is asked when they tell someone they're a writer. It's a simple question but surprisingly hard for some writers to answer, especially first-timers. In fact, some writers often launch into a lengthy description of what their book is about, when what the asker really wants to know is the genre.

Genre is determined by four things: plot, story, character, and setting. The way each of these elements are crafted into a story and how they come together will determine what genre a book falls into.

Classical literature is sometimes broken into five major genres: contemporary fiction, historical fiction, science fiction, fantasy, and mystery, while nonfiction can be described as: descriptive, persuasive, narrative, and expository. Notice our use of the words "sometimes" and "can be." We use these words because genres are changing as fast as the technologies used to organize books and literature are changing. Database organization, keywords, hashtags, metadata, and indexes have a profound impact on what different organizations related to the publishing industry would call genre.

For instance, libraries rely on the Dewey decimal system to group books into ten general classifications: general works; philosophy and psychology; religion; social sciences; language; natural sciences and mathematics; technology; arts; literature and rhetoric; and history, biography, and geography. In contrast, the International Standard Book Number (ISBN) association Bowker, which is where ISBNs are assigned to books published in the United States, lists ninety genres or subjects. Wikipedia's List of Literary Genres is several hundred genres long, often going into extreme detail such as Amish romance and splatterpunk horror. You can probably surmise from the evocative title of that last one *exactly* what you're going to read in that genre.

In short, it depends on where you get your information as to what the list of genres looks like, and new genres continue to be created as writers find new ways to tell their stories. For instance, anime and graphic novels are relatively new to many readers, with anime emerging in the mid-1950s and graphic novels gaining popularity in the late 1970s. Amish romance originated in the 1990s and splatterpunk in the 1980s.

Listen, we're not going to tell you that genre is Super Important in the way other items about your work are—such as, oh, plot or character development—but it's still something you might think about as you're writing your novel. You don't need to think *too* hard about it, just enough to know what the genre is and the possible ways it can affect your project and the decisions you make about it, which is what this chapter is primarily about.

It's actually entirely possible to write your book without paying any attention to genre at all until you have to list it somewhere—because even Amazon will ask you to pick a genre. What we want to impart in this chapter is that genre helps form certain expectations about how a story will unfold, so knowing what those expectations are will help you as you make your way through writing that first draft, during pre-marketing, and especially when you get into querying, pitching, and the serious marketing of your book.

What's It All About?

Genre exists for a reason. It creates expectations between readers and writers.

When a writer says they write steampunk Westerns, a reader knows the story will contain a Western theme with unusual machines and possibly be somewhat speculative, i.e. aspects that don't exist in reality. A steampunk Western romance will have all of that but also follow a romance plot and probably, but not always, end in a happily ever after.

Libraries use genre to classify where to put a book. Before digital cataloging was even a dream in a tech-nerd's head, librarians used the Dewey decimal system to place books in an order that could be taught and used across the entire system. That's why it doesn't matter whether you're walking into a library in the smallest town in Nebraska or in the huge metropolis of New York City, all you have to do is look in the 398.2 section to find your favorite fairy tale.

As we moved into the digital age and books became searchable in other ways, the idea of genre was still considered necessary to bookstores, publishers, and online e-stores as a way of reaching readers looking for stories in certain categories. A mystery lover can, with a great deal of success, walk into a bookstore and be surrounded by mysteries.

The popular opinion about genre is that if you want to brand yourself, you have to stick to one genre. We just heard the shaking of heads of the thousands of authors who have successfully branded themselves as writers of multiple genres. However, there are a lot of reasons this is good advice, especially for writers just starting out. Finding and sticking to a genre gives you the chance to perfect the expected conventions of that genre. If, for example, you write exclusively in the romance genre, your experience with reading and writing in that genre will help hone your skills in creating a solid work that romance readers will love. Each genre has certain conventions a reader comes to expect in that genre. Writing in one genre exclusively allows you to master those conventions. By the way, our strong belief is that the best writers are voracious readers. One of the best ways to really get to know a genre is to read it, especially in the early stages of writing in it.

Another compelling argument for writing in one genre (and to underscore what we talked about in the previous chapter) is it makes it easier to create and maintain your branding. Author Melissa Brayden's tagline is "Love. Laughter. Books." She writes heartwarming, sexy, funny, women-loving-women romances. Her readers have come to expect this. They know that if they read a book by Brayden, they're getting a good story that they'll come away from smiling. That's a brand.

And that's not a bad thing. If you're going to be known for something, being known as a master of lighthearted romances is certainly more specific to audiences than being known as that eclectic author who writes a lot of weird stuff. In this case, sticking with one genre is helpful to the author in gaining readers by establishing their trust regarding what they're going to receive. This helps readers who have strong tastes and want to know what they're getting when they pick up a book. Some readers count on that trust and will feel betrayed when it's broken. Betrayal leads to bad reviews, and no one wants that.

Publishers love genres. How much easier is it to say, "This author writes high fantasy stories" than it is to say, "This author writes something we're not even sure how to classify—but it's good. Trust us."

Now, before all those successful multi-genre writing authors get whiplash from shaking their heads, there is no unbreakable rule about sticking to one genre. If you choose to write in multiple genres, it's good to know the reasons it's easier to pick one genre. Having this information will prepare you for the challenges you may face and allow you to pre-emptively create solutions.

Of course, the list of genres is ever-growing, and blended genres are becoming more popular. For instance, check out this description of *The Martian Chronicles* by Ray Bradbury in the article by Lincoln Michel, *The 10 Best Genre-Bending Books* in the Nov 13, 2015, *Publisher's Weekly*:

> *On its surface, The Martian Chronicles seems to fit squarely in the science fiction camp. But the loosely connected novel—really separate short stories that were later combined—has none of the world-building or serious examination of technology that we normally think of as SF. The Martians, for example, change powers and personality as the stories of various tone and length go along. Instead, the underlying story of humanity's invasion and colonization of Mars allows Bradbury to tell a wide variety of tales. Some are cerebral comedies that could have been written by Donald Barthelme or Italo Calvino, while others are beautifully written tales of heartbreak and nostalgia. Elements of horror, dystopia, and political allegory also seep into this essential SF book.*

Ultimately, the book is considered science fiction, but Bradbury weaves in comedy, romance, dystopia, horror, and other genres.

A wide range of books with blended genres are currently popular. There are vampire romances, science fiction murder mystery, historical crime dramas, and ancient Greek selkie pirate dinosaurs. (Okay, we may have made that last one up, but you're welcome to use the idea!) The point is that there are a lot of ways to classify your novel these days, but it will best advantage your marketing to have a main genre in which you list your work.

Someone with a strong base in selling romance books is more likely to be put at the front of the list for promotion than someone who is all over the board. Audiences get recommendations based on past purchases, so someone who exclusively buys young adult speculative fiction is going to see recommendations for young adult speculative fiction in targeted digital advertising when they go online. If you exclusively write young adult speculative fiction, your books will eventually end up making it to the recommendations for folks who buy in that genre. If you suddenly produce a queer romance, that book may, or may not, show up in front of your established readers.

Truth Bomb: The authors of this book read and write in different genres, and some of our favorite authors do the same. We absolutely understand the advice about sticking to one genre, and we understand how it helps to establish a strong writing career. However, by now, you know our stance on absolutes. There is no one-size-fits-all in writing. You can do whatever you want as long as you can do it well.

To tie this up, an author can choose to stick to one genre, or they can write in multiple genres, even blending genres in a single book. All of these options can be incredibly successful. However, there can be drawbacks such as confusion when expectations aren't met, the possible dilution of a fanbase, and probably the worst thing—readers may get angry if they expect one thing and get another. But your story is the most important factor. Having a basic understanding of the qualities of various genres as you're writing will help you make decisions to avoid the drawbacks.

Summary

In terms of planning your book, genre isn't the most important thing to think about, but it does factor into many decisions you ultimately make in the course of writing and promoting your book. Most of the time, you will already have a good idea about what genre you are working in, so the main thing is to understand the expectations that come with the genre and to be aware of when and why you are deviating from these expectations. Finally, the choices you make in regard to genre may have an impact on clarity when discussing your work with important people such as publishers and readers, managing your readership, and establishing your brand.

Frequently Asked Questions

If I write in different genres, do I need a new pen name for each one?

Need? Not necessarily. *Want?* Maybe.

This is the single question that prompted us to add genre as a planning point in this book. At one time in publishing history, the answer would have been a solid yes. As we mentioned earlier in this chapter, libraries and bookstores organized books by genre, and it was a very manual process. Another compelling reason was that publishers were, and still are to a certain extent, insistent on staying true to brand, and genre is a big part of most authors' brands. However, some would argue that both reasons have become less important, especially in the last ten years or so with digital organization making the discovery of books by new readers much easier. The success of many well-known authors who have ventured into multiple genres has also been a big factor in making working in a single genre less important to readers and publishing entities.

Some things to keep in mind regarding multiple pen names would be: your desire for privacy; the appeal to most large publishing houses, which lean toward authors writing in a single genre; whether the genres you are writing in are aimed at two audiences that should remain separated, such as erotica and children's books; the time it takes to maintain multiple identities; your ability to keep the personas separate; and your ability to produce work in multiple genres—just to name a few.

Can my book have multiple genres?

Yes. Many do. One of our favorite blended books is *Pride and Prejudice and Zombies*. It's romance, comedy, horror, action, and historical fiction all rolled into one.

What genre do I pick if the place I'm listing my book requires one genre and my story contains two genres? For instance, my story is mostly funny about a battle that takes place in space with a romance between a human and a being from another galaxy.

First of all, we want to read this story! Second of all, pick the dominant genre. Is the space battle the primary arc? Or the romance? The less-dominant arc will be the sub-genre, which is something most book databases and book sites include. If there isn't a dominant arc, pick the one you like the best or the one you think will have the greatest appeal.

Recommended Resources

Okay, resource police, please don't tar and feather us. We know Wikipedia.com is not the best resource when it comes to many things, because it isn't always correct due to the community sourcing of information. However, it has the single most comprehensive list of genres we have found, and the list continues to grow as new genres are created.

https://en.wikipedia.org/wiki/List_of_writing_genres

Discussion Time

Finnian and Kimberly talk about genres.

Go here to watch the video: https://youtu.be/YzH4qWHES04

Try it Yourself

Take one of the following prompts and write three short stories: one as a drama or action, one as a comedy or romance, and one combining both genres you chose.

- A kindhearted doctor struggles to find the cure for their patient's rare disease, and the clock is ticking.

- It is a case of mistaken identity, a suitcase filled with money, and a chance to redeem themselves.

- A group of strangers is stranded in a desolate place, and it requires teamwork to find their way back home.

- When their dream of greatness is shattered, they have to pick up the pieces and learn to live again.

- A walk in the woods reveals a mysterious item.

Plot and Outlining

Plot—A plot is made up of the central events that affect the outcome of the story and the outline. Another way to say it is that the plot is what the story is about, and the outline is comprised of all of the events that support it. When used together, the plot and outline help map out the way the story is told.

Outline—An outline is the set of elements that make up the overall structure of the story and is often used as a tool to plan a story, keep track of events, and provide an at-a-glance summary of the story so they don't always need to dig through the manuscript—which keeps getting longer and longer—to find something they need to reference.

We have combined both plot and outline in one chapter because they are so closely integrated during the planning process. We thought it would be useful to see them working together, and because the story arc is so closely related, we threw it in, too.

Story Arc—Also known as the **narrative arc**, the story arc is the **structure and shape** of a story. It is made up of the events in the story and includes the plot, setting, conflict, characters, and theme.

While we're defining elements related to plot and outline, you may have heard the term "beat sheet" in the same context as plotting and outlining, so we'll throw this one in for your delight:

Beat Sheet—An abbreviated type of outlining (originally designed by American screenwriter, Blake Snyder) that some authors use to chart their story. Like an outline, the beat sheet gives a chronological flow of the story, but it is different in that it is comprised of brief bullet points with little detail. In this way, the points are the "beats" the author needs to hit in order to convey the essential, and probably most emotional, points in the story.

> *All fiction is about people, unless it's about rabbits pretending to be people. It's all essentially characters in action, which means characters moving through time and changes taking place, and that's what we call 'the plot.'* —**Margaret Atwood**

Introduction

If you're currently a pantser, that is, someone who just opens a document and starts writing a book without any kind of outlining, you may be tempted to skip this chapter. After all, if you can just bust out a novel without having to think about the gory details of character arcs, elements of plot, and loose ends, why waste time trying to suss all those things out? We get it. You want to jump into the deep end and start swimming. You want to do the fun stuff and skip the drudgery. You're the person who picks up a violin and wants to play a concerto without doing scales.

Us too!

But this is a book about planning, and outlining can be the difference between plot holes big enough to eat a car and a tight, fast-paced, and enthralling book that keeps your reader on the edge of their seat from start to finish. Will the bad guy get their due? Will the protagonist find the prize? Did your character meet an important person in chapter three who saves the day in chapter sixteen? Will the main characters have a happily ever after?

These are the things you need to know about your book. So, let's talk about it.

What It's All About

There are writers, especially series writers, with legions of characters and entire worlds to keep track of, who spend years plotting their novels. We're not suggesting you spend years writing your outline. We're suggesting you should do yourself the favor of spending some time now, in the beginning, to work out your plot to save yourself writer's block, loose ends, and unnecessary characters later. It isn't going to hurt you to take several hours or even a few weeks to construct a powerful outline that will later give you the freedom to spend time with the passion part of the story while the framework holds it together.

A note about Pantsers vs. Plotters: While we spend considerable time in this chapter talking about planning an outline, we don't think pantsers are doing it wrong. In fact, we're in awe of pantsers and have even been pantsers at various points in our writing experience. The thing is, whether you do a formal outline before you start or just go with the story in your head, the outline happens; it's just that one happens before the story comes to life, and the other happens in real time.

With that said, before we get into the technicalities of outlining, let's talk about one of the biggest misconceptions surrounding it.

MYTH: Outlining my book will stifle my creativity

Give us a second here, and we'll dispel this fallacy. First, go to https://youtu.be/qGuOZPwLayY and watch the movie trailer for *Castaway*. You've now spent three minutes of your life watching an outline. Think about it.

The **basic premise** of an outline is this:

1. **Setup** showing the character's current real world

2. The **inciting incident** that leads the character to a new normal

3. The main character's goal(s) or **desire**(s)

4. The main character's primary **opponent**

5. The **rising action** where obstacles are introduced, preventing the character from getting what they want, finally coming to a moment where the reader fears all is lost

6. The **climax** when the character overcomes all

7. The **resolution** or dénouement

Comparing the *Castaway* movie trailer with the above, we can ascertain the following plot points:

1. **Setup**—We get to see the main character's life as a FedEx exec and his loving relationship with his partner.

2. **Inciting Incident**—He's thrust into a predicament when the plane crashes, leaving him stranded on a deserted island.

3. **Goals/Desires**—His goals are first to survive and next to get off the island.

4. **Opponent**—His primary opponent is the island, and to a lesser extent his own mind.

5. **Rising Action**—Obstacles such as extreme loneliness, hunger, and the need to make shelter and find food are thrown at him.

6. **Climax**—We even see the extreme moment leading up to the climax—Chuck Noland decides to take his chance on getting off the island on a homemade raft.

7. **Resolution**—The only thing we don't know from this trailer is the resolution, but since we're optimists and we've seen a lot of movies, we can bet he's going to make it off the island. Whether he gets to resume his former "real" life is up in the air.

How can the movie producers afford to show us every level of the plot of this movie and still trust that we're going to want to see it? For the same reason you can outline your entire novel and still trust that your reader is going to want to read it. The story. The characters. The flesh and blood of your work. We know that almost every great novel we've loved follows the same basic plot arc, yet we still read them because the way they get to those points draws us in. The characters come to life. The story unfolds. *Star Wars* and *Harry Potter* may have the same basic structure, but they are not the same story. Not at all.

Your freedom comes in how you tell the story. It's in Chuck Noland dancing around the fire, making friends with a volleyball, and finally deciding to become his own hero. It's the ghost parties, shifting staircases, and house elves at Hogwarts. It's the fact that your main character has a stutter, and it makes a reappearance when she tries to talk to the love interest. It's the life you bring to your work.

"But wait," you say. "I'm writing a romance, contemporary fiction, or a memoir. While this plot arc might be true for action movies and fantasy stories, it doesn't apply to me." Surprisingly enough, it does. So, let's look at another movie trailer.

Watch the trailer for *The Photograph*. https://youtu.be/954b9vLAT6Y Now apply what you saw to the above-mentioned basic plot premise, and you get this:

1. **Setup**—We get a glimpse of the main character's real world of working, living the single life as a strong independent person, with great friends.

2. **Inciting Incident**—The hot photographer comes to talk about her mother's work and awkwardly asks her out in a super-charming way, kicking off the story.

3. **Goals/Desires**—Her goals change as she struggles with how to share space with her new boyfriend while redefining what happiness means and how relationships work.

4. **Opponent**—The main conflict here is person-against-herself. The main character is her own worst enemy.

5. **Rising Action**—She throws up her own obstacles by alienating her love interest out of fear of commitment, lack of trust, and worry about being too much like her mother.

6. **Climax**—Finally, she pushes him away, and he makes a grand gesture to get her back.

7. **Resolution**—The resolution is a mystery since it's the trailer, so we don't know for sure, but since this is a love story, we can guess how it turns out.

Now that we've done this with two very different movies, you will never be able to unsee how trailers give us pretty much the entire outline. Go to any movie trailer or think of any great book you've read recently, and you'll probably be able to determine the 7-point plot structure. Look for the setup seen as the established world, the inciting incident, the main goal or desire, the opponent, the rising action or the obstacles, the climax, and the resolution.

There is still plenty the trailers don't tell us. There are subplots and individual character arcs, the supporting scenes and interesting details that make the story rich. So, anyone telling you that working from an outline stifles creativity is probably someone who hasn't created one for a book they've written. They're discounting a valuable tool.

A note about subplots… If you watched the above-mentioned movie trailers, you'll notice that we also saw a little bit of the "B" story in each of these trailers. While Chuck Noland's main goal is to survive and ultimately get off the island, we get glimpses of the love story in the background. In *The Photograph*, the romance is the main plot, but we also catch a bit of the mystery surrounding the main character's mother and her disappearance.

Subplots are a great way to add depth to a story. They can add detail and backstory, show motivation, add to the tension, and immerse the reader in a complex and compelling world. Subplots, like the main plot, follow the same 7-Point plot structure that moves the reader along. So, when you add subplots into your story, remember to apply the 7-Point plot structure to them, albeit with less detail, and, very importantly, make sure they provide additional and necessary information to the main plot, otherwise they will detract from your story and probably confuse your reader. We'll talk more about this a little later in this chapter.

Now, back to our discussion about plots in general…

The more you understand about plot, the more you will realize that, regardless of the theme of the story, all plots follow the same basic path with just a few changes depending on the genre and the plot structure chosen, which we'll talk about in the following sections of this chapter. But if you're trying to figure out how to write your story, and you're not sure how to get started on an outline, try doing this simple exercise.

Exercise: Plot—Getting Started

1. Introduce your character by creating an opening scene where your character is in their current situation/setting. Give an idea of what their basic dissatisfaction or end goal is. Some examples could be a character living a boring life and wishing for adventure, a character who has spent their life avoiding love because of their trust issues, or a fisherman going out to sea to catch some fish. The setup is the character's status quo. It's Harry living in the cupboard under the stairs in *Harry Potter and the Sorcerer's Stone*. It's Iris being in love with her jerk ex-lover in *The Holiday*.

   Example: Kyrie and her parents live in tents in the Forest of Alnight in the foothills of the mountains at the end of the empire. The empire is at war, royalty has been deposed, their magic has been bound, leaving them with little defense, and factions are fighting. An overlord, an evil dictator, sits in the castle at Gorn. People are starving in the empire and being killed for minor offenses. Kyrie and her parents are part of a rebel faction seeking to restore the benevolent monarchy and bring peace back to the kingdom. They move their tent village from place to place when the Shadow Hunters escalate their attacks, and the Shadow Hunters have started another escalation. The village is restless. Kyrie patrols with the sentries, watching for attacks.

2. Describe an incident that will cause your character to have to make a change during the course of the story. This could be meeting another character, a crossover into a new world, or maybe a decision to do something wild and take an overseas trip to get over a bad lover. It could be meeting a mentor figure, who convinces the main character to try something new.

Example: Kyrie turns twenty-five, her year of individuation, and her mother takes her aside and tells her they are the true rulers of the empire. Tells her the family's magic amulet was stolen by a traitor to the empire during the Twelve-day Assault, driving the empire to war, forcing Kyrie's family into hiding, and binding the magic of anyone who will not swear allegiance to Maxis. Kyrie's parents tell her the Dimness is on the verge of draining the empire of its life force, and it is up to her to travel across the land, disguise herself as a member of one of the rival factions, and steal the amulet back.

3. Identify your character's goal. Your character might have more than one goal. They may want to save the small-town bookstore, fall in love with the hot lumberjack, and raise their child to be a happy, healthy person. Maybe they want to save the space station and catch the eye of the cute alien who just transferred onboard. Your character's goals may change through the course of your novel. They may start off thinking they want to solve the murder case and/or make that journey, but along the way they come to realize they want so much more than that. Many of these plot points come from the character arc, which we will dive deeper into in the Character Sketches chapter. For now, just think about your character's main goals as you understand them at this point in your planning.

    Example: Our main character needs to regain Castle Gorn and free the land from the Dimness. All of her life, she has had the same dream each night in which she goes on a great journey to reclaim her family's rightful place in Castle Gorn, which was taken by Maxis in the Twelve-day Assault, and to restore her mother's rule over Gornheld. But she is afraid that she will not succeed, that more will die in the process, and that she will never see her parents again.

4. Define the main character's primary opponent in the story. While there may be other plot points that get in the way of your main character's success, this opponent will be the penultimate challenge your character needs to win in order to obtain their goal. Often the opponent is a specific person or thing, such as a monster or a bully, but it can also be a metaphorical idea such as "the demons in your mind" or "chasing windmills" for the main character to overcome. Many opponents in stories can be reoccurring literary themes, also known as tropes. Examples of tropes are: "man against nature," "love always wins," "enemies to friends," "evil will be vanquished," etc. There are seemingly countless tropes. Some critics will talk about tropes as if they're something to be avoided, but they can't be avoided. In fact, most stories are made up of multiple tropes. The idea is to try to approach the trope you're writing about in a unique way.

Example: In previous examples, we have walked through a fabricated story about The Shadow Hunters. Using that example, one could imagine that the trope is "the rightful heir," which would make the opponent the evil dictator who stole the empire.

5. Come up with three to five events that prevent your character from reaching their goal. These create the necessary tension your reader needs to stay interested in the story. Even if the reader is pretty sure the character will get what they want in the end, they want to see what the character overcomes in order to get it. If the character is trying to save the small-town bookstore, maybe the obstacles are failing sales, a big city businessman who wants to open a large bookstore franchise in the town square, or the zoning commission refusing to allow the business to reopen until the building is completely renovated. Maybe your main character is trying to prevent the space station from being destroyed, and the obstacles are a marauding band of alien ruffians who seem one step ahead of her every time. Maybe she's also fighting PTSD from the time she caused the shuttle accident that killed her father. These events should build up to a point at which the reader will think there's a chance the character will not overcome the problem. Besides being interesting for the reader, obstacles provide an opportunity to reveal things about your character that might not be revealed when things are going along as normal.

Example:

- The village seer tells Kyrie and her travel companion that one of them will not return from the journey.

- They run into the Shadow Hunters.

- Eldric, a Shadow Hunter, pretends to be a fellow traveler and befriends them. All Shadow Hunters are non-binary, removing an aspect that might be used to divide them in battle.

- Soteria (Kyrie's best friend and travel companion) is killed when they enter the castle, and Kyrie gives up and leaves without defeating the evil dictator.

6. Determine a satisfying climax in which the character reaches their ultimate goal. Edward climbs the fire escape in *Pretty Woman*, cementing his love true love for Vivian. All but two soldiers are killed in the quest to save Private Ryan. It's the real Keyser Soze exiting the police station at the end of *The Usual Suspects*, leaving both the police detective and the audience catching their breath as they realize the truth.

Example: Kyrie fights and defeats Skarsgard and Maxis, restoring rule of the empire to Kyrie's family.

7. Note your falling action and resolution. In most books, this is the last few pages. This is where you'll wrap up the last hanging threads and ensure everyone finishes feeling satisfied.

The empress is reinstated in Castle Gorn, and the empire begins to heal. A major celebration, with a memorial for Soteria, takes place.

Common Plot Structures

Plot structure refers to the basic sequence of events that tell a story. Quite a bit of energy has been invested by literary types throughout history on defining the best way to tell a story, resulting in different structures such as Freytag's Pyramid, the 3-Act Structure, the 5-Act Structure, The Hero's Journey, and others. Some were developed in an attempt to explain the components and patterns of often-used structures, and others to provide a specific way to build the best stories.

Our previous analysis for the movie trailers follows the 3-Act Structure, but you will recognize elements that appear in all the structures we'll explore in the next few pages.

Freytag's Pyramid

One of the most well-known and simplest plot structures you may have heard of is Freytag's Pyramid, which we've adapted into the image below, and which is the core of our own Story Arc Worksheet.

Story Arc Worksheet

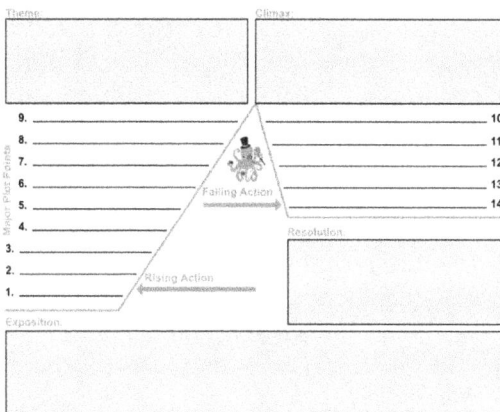

my inkslinger

Theme:

Climax:

The Story Arc

Exposition: Introduces the main character(s) to the reader, tells what problem is to be solved, and sets the place and tone. Main character(s) and problem to be solved, inciting incident, setting time, setting place.

9. _____
8. _____
7. _____
6. _____
5. _____
4. _____
3. _____
2. _____
1. _____

10.
11.
12.
13.
14.

Major Plot Points

Falling Action

Resolution:

Rising Action

Exposition:

Rising Action: The build up of tension to the climax explaining what the story is about and contains the inciting incident.

Climax: This is the main character(s)' moment of truth.

Falling Action: Describes the consequences to the actions of the character(s), tying up loose ends.

Resolution: How the story ends, closing the loop of the story.

inkstacks.com/inkslinger/story-arc

Gustav Freytag was a 19TH century playwright, who created a structure for dramatic plots or tragedies. While this structure is not ideal for all story types, it does contain the five main elements of most stories: introduction, rising action (Freytag called this the *rising movement*), climax, falling action, and resolution.

A wonderful aspect of Freytag's Pyramid is its visual representation of the emotional arc of a story. Freytag is known to have based his pyramid on the 5-Act Structure, which we will briefly talk about next.

The 5-Act Structure

Some credit the Roman poet Horace with creating the 5-Act Structure, while some say Aristotle or even Shakespeare created it. However it was Gustav Freytag who made the structure popular in more recent times.

Act I—Introduction

This act contains the setup and the inciting incident.

Contains approximately the first 10% of the story.

Act II—The Rising Action

This act consists of the events that move the story toward the climax.

Contains approximately 35% to 40% of the story.

Act III—Climax

This act is the apex of tension in the story, where everything comes to the final crisis.

Contains less than 10% of the story, often occurring in a single scene.

Act IV—Falling Action

This act starts with the climax, contains all the scenes that lead to the resolution, and describes the results of the actions taken prior, often including doubt that the main characters will get what they desire.

Contains approximately 25 to 30% of the story.

Act V—Catastrophe

This act is the resolution of the story or, because the 5-Act Structure is designed for dramas and tragedies, this is where everyone dies, and the protagonist gets what's coming to them. When used for a comedy or romance, the main character gets the thing they want, or the happily ever after occurs.

Contains 10% or less of the story.

In reviewing the 5-Act Structure, one thing stands out: the climax occurs in the middle of the story. This doesn't seem to match up with many contemporary stories, which tells us that the original intention of this structure has shifted a bit to move the climax and ensuing acts to the last 25% of the story. This just goes to show you that literary constructs are a really good guide but can be adjusted for the benefit of the storyteller when needed.

The Hero's Journey

Another well-known structure is in prolific writer, editor, and mythology scholar Joseph Campbell's depiction of what he called *The Hero's Journey*. This plot structure is a useful plot path for action/fantasy fiction.

The Hero's Journey

Departure	1. **The call to adventure**—the inciting action that inspires the hero (protagonist) to act. 2. **Refusal of the call**—the hero may not acknowledge the call at first, or decide they don't want to answer it. 3. **Supernatural aid**—the coincidental help of an outside nature that urges the hero to act. 4. **The crossing of the first threshold**—the first step of many that leads the hero through the adventure. 5. **Belly of the whale**—this is a reference to Pinocchio or Jonah, where the hero has moved past the point of return and begins a transformation, finally accepting the call.

Initiation	1. **The road of trials**—this is the set of ordeals the hero must overcome on their journey.
	2. **The meeting with the goddess**—the hero first encounters or becomes aware of the thing that matters to them most of all, usually love, even if it is for themselves.
	3. **Woman as the temptress**—this represents the temptations the hero encounters that might lead them away from their journey or quest.
	4. **Atonement with the parent**—the hero faces the thing that has the most power over them and gains atonement or acknowledgement.
	5. **Apotheosis**—the hero has become god-like.
	6. **The ultimate boon**—the goal of the quest has been met.

Return	1. **Refusal of the return**—having accomplished their mission, the hero may not want to return to where they began, there may be other issues to attend to, strings to tie up. 2. **The magic flight**—having obtained the goal, it might be used to obtain closure on other aspects of the journey. 3. **Rescue from without**—the hero may be injured emotionally or physically, and the appearance of a mentor or guide helps them get back to their home. 4. **The crossing of the return threshold**—the hero returns and teaches the world what they learned on their quest. 5. **Master of the two worlds**—balance has been achieved for the hero. 6. **Freedom to live**—the hero has overcome the obstacles and now has the confidence to move on.

The 3-Act Structure

One of the most versatile plot structures is the 3-Act Structure. It has been suggested that Aristotle originally referred to the 3-Act Structure in his analysis of storytelling, and it has been a structure referred to and used by playwrights and story writers ever since. It elaborates on the premise that all stories should have a distinct beginning, middle, and end, and that each act consists of specific plot points, telling a balanced story. This structure has been used for so long that readers have come to expect the stories they read to follow this general sequence of events. The 3-Act structure has become a foundation of most other literary structures, and you can see its influence when you study them. We'll go over some of the other structures in the following pages.

The purpose of the 3-Act Structure is to provide a map of the basic plot points of a story, arranged in a specific sequence, which gives the story a comfortable cadence. Each plot point weaves together to propel the story forward in an expected fashion until a satisfying conclusion. When using this structure, a writer can compose their story in an easy flow, maintaining their creativity, while ensuring they don't miss a critical element of the plot. This structure also makes it easy to deconstruct the story to look for issues when a completed story just doesn't seem to work.

While there are three acts in this structure, it is generally accepted that the first act takes about 25% of the story, the second act takes up about 50%, and the end takes up the remaining 25%.

The 3-Act Structure

Act I	Act II	Act III
Setup	The Choice	The Climax
Inciting incident	Obstacles	Falling Action
Introduction of side-characters and subplots	Relief	Processing
The debate/second thoughts	More obstacles	Last revelations
Beginning—25% of the story	Absolute disaster	Dénouement
	Middle—50% of the story	**End—25% of the story**

In each case, there is a beginning, a middle, and an end, and they all have a rising action (events) toward a major crisis culminating in the climax, followed by a falling action. The rising action is what builds the tension, making the story compelling, and the falling action provides a sense of relief and closure.

You can look at rising action like this: each new obstacle should seem bigger and more insurmountable than the last, but there are brief moments in between when the character starts to believe they're actually going to make it. This allows the reader to take a breath, and it gives the writer an opportunity to show what the main character is made of. This technique is called scene and sequel. Using this technique, a writer uses scenes where the character is faced with obstacles while moving the story forward toward the character's goals. At the end of each scene, the sequel occurs where the character reacts to and analyzes what happened in the scene, resulting in the character's decision about what to do next.

Using scene and sequel, your character will be stumbling and picking themselves back up. It's almost dying in the wall of fire in *The Hunger Games* then meeting Rue, who helps Katniss defeat the other teams hunting them. It's Rue dying but District 11 sending help because Katniss treated Rue with respect and love.

In *The Holiday*, it's Iris and Miles starting to realize they have feelings for each other, but Miles is still entwined with his not-so-great girlfriend.

In *The Princess Bride*, it's Wesley and Buttercup surviving rodents of unusual size and taking a few moments to hug and celebrate before they're captured by Prince Humperdink.

The tension keeps on rising until the crisis occurs and the climax decides the fates of the main characters. After which the reader's heart rate begins to go back to normal during the falling action, when in every book and movie ever made comes the explanation of why the story was told, whether it is the villain getting what was coming to them, the hero or heroine riding off into the sunset, the moral of the story being brought home, or the star-crossed lovers realizing that love overcomes everything.

This is why Freytag's Pyramid is a little too simplistic and Campbell's Hero's Journey focuses on overcoming different challenges along the path—you don't just have one giant wall of rising action; you have peaks and valleys to tease the tension upward until the climax comes with the big bang. Then everyone gets to breathe a little and figure out what it was all about. If you do it right, your story will stick with the reader for a long time after they put your book down.

We know what you're thinking now: "As brilliant and as good-looking as you two are, stop with all the boring details that made me drool across my desk in high school already! What structure should I use?"

We're big fans of the basic 3-Act structure. It's simple. It encompasses most of the nuances of each plot structure without being specific to any one genre. It can be traced back to Aristotle and was a favored structure by Shakespeare. You could say it's withstood the test of time.

So, yeah, the 3-Act Structure is the one we'd suggest in most instances.

Now that you know what plot structure we prefer, let's get into a little more detail about it. Grab a snack and your favorite beverage, and in the next few pages, we'll go over what each element in each act is, why they exist where they do, and how they progress the story.

Act I: The Beginning

The Setup

The setup begins with the opening scene then proceeds with telling, or hinting at, why the story is being told. In most plot structures, it shows one or more characters' regular life and gives an indication that there's some dissatisfaction or at least a problem that needs to be fixed. This is what gets the reader invested. In *The Wizard of Oz*, it's Dorothy being bored with Kansas. In *Bridesmaids*, it's Annie Walker being forced to sneak out of her casual sex partner Ted's house and climbing over the security gate because he asked her to leave her after sex and she's tired of being his booty call.

It makes sense that the setup should be at the very beginning of the story because it keeps the reader from wondering why the character is doing all the things they are doing as the story progresses. Plus, a story has to start somewhere, right? This is where you plop your reader right into the thick of things, give them an outcome to hope for, and make them so curious about what comes next, they can't put the book down.

The Inciting Incident

In a non-romance, it's the moment that triggers the chain of events that takes the main character from their status quo life into a quest to fulfil their dream. In *Harry Potter and the Sorcerer's Stone*, it's Hagrid barging into the hut in which the family has hidden on Harry's birthday. In *The Hunger Games,* it's the moment Katniss's sister is chosen as tribute and Katniss volunteers to take her place. The inciting incident doesn't have to be huge. In *Black Panther*, it's when T'Challa is crowned king and fights with the man from the neighboring tribe to prove his worth. In all cases, it's the moment that begins the change of the main character's life from what it was to what it is going to be. In a romance, this could also be when the two protagonists meet, sometimes referred to as the **meet cute** but not always. In *The Holiday*, the inciting incident occurs separately for each character when they realize they need a break, and they agree to switch houses. In *Sleepless in Seattle*, for Sam Baldwin, it's the moment he calls into the radio show and talks about his dead wife.

In the movie *The Holiday*, there are two meet cutes—one between Graham and Amanda, when Amanda asks Graham to have unfettered/non-committal vacation sex with her, and the other in LA, where Iris meets Miles, who is being super funny but also in a relationship with someone who is absolutely horrible for him. In *The Photograph*, it's the second time Mae and Michael meet, and it's Michael, Mr. Hot Photographer, being uber-adorable as he awkwardly asks out Mae.

The inciting incident is the story's catalyst. It sets everything in motion. It's the realization that something has to change. It's the point where everything goes out of balance, forcing the main characters to act. It's also a common place to start establishing your characters' flaws because a big part of the character arc is the main character's transformation from who they start out as in the beginning of the story to who they become in the end.

Having the inciting incident after the setup makes sense because it can save the writer from having to backtrack and explain why these characters have been chosen to go on this journey.

> **Truth Bomb:** An important note about ACT I: you are going to establish your **theme** in this act. It could be that "There is always a second chance at love" or "You have to be true to yourself to find the one" or in

The Hunger Games, it's simply "survival". There are all kinds of themes, and most stories have more than one, but you get the picture, right? This is where it's introduced, and this is what the reader will be interested in seeing built upon throughout the story, until the character achieves their goal at the end of the story. So, the Super Important thing to note here is to make sure the theme is clear, and the entire story is centered around it until it is resolved.

While most writers start with a general idea of what their story is about, sometimes it's hard for them to define the theme. Don't worry. As you're writing, the theme will probably become apparent to you.

Subplots and Most Secondary Characters

We talked a little about subplots earlier, but subplots and secondary characters add a level of pizazz to a story. These are usually introduced in Act I. The thing to remember here is that main characters normally do not exist in a vacuum. They have other people in their lives who have their own stories running in parallel to the main story, and who work to make the story and main characters more interesting. They also give the main characters opportunities to show their uniqueness and why they're worth learning more about. Because all elements of the story are used to progress the main plot, you must make sure the subplots and side characters are instrumental in either developing your main character or increasing the tension in the storyline. For those reasons, Act I is a good time to introduce these side stories and supporting characters.

An example of a side story could be in a drama in which the main story is about saving a space station from malicious destruction, but there's a subplot of a boss who's trying to fire the main character because the main character sometimes takes the boss's parking place. This side story can really ramp up the tension because the reader feels protective of the main character having to deal with mundane career issues caused by their jerk of a boss while also trying to save all the people on the space station, which, by the way, also has a cure for a disease on it, which the clueless boss isn't aware of, but it just so happens his kid needs it or they will die. Whew! We really got into that one. Our heart is pounding. Stupid boss… Anyway, maybe their best friend is dealing with an attempt to recruit them into a rebel alliance, too, and the main character is trying to prevent that.

As you can see, subplots can make the story more interesting. They can also distract the reader from the main story if you're not careful. In that case, we might take the parking space thing out. Yes, it gives a motive for the boss's dislike of the main character, but then we need to explain why our main character is into pushing the boss's buttons, and we don't want the reader wondering about that when there's a space station to be saved.

The Debate/Second Thoughts

This part comes near the end of the first act, and this is the point in the story where the main character decides whether or not they will face the main challenge of the story. This is the beginning of building real tension in the story. Will they, or won't they? Do they go on the first date? Does the superhero don the formfitting suit? Does Harry go through the secret door on Platform 9 ¾? These questions are almost always theoretical. We know the answer will always be yes because, otherwise, there would be no story, right? The reason for the debate/second thoughts is that it provides more information about the characters. Are they eager to face it? Do they try to get out of it? Are they forced to make a choice, like Katniss in *The Hunger Games*? They will do it, but the way in which they set forth often creates a decisive tone to the story. It not only conveys who they are as a person but what kind of transformation they will undergo by the story's end.

Okay, so Act I involves setting the story up, giving clues about what to expect, and providing the reader with a reason to be invested in the story.

Act II: The Middle

Act II contains the bulk of your story. The rising action takes place in this act and will take the story all the way to the climax, which starts Act III. You may have heard writers lament about the mushy middle, where the storytelling might get difficult and the writer has a hard time because they didn't plan enough obstacles for their characters. Because this section contains most of the action, you should continue moving the story forward while including more information about your characters, building tension, and layering the story to give it more depth. Think of Katniss meeting the tracker jackers and Forrest Gump being sent to Vietnam as Jenny tells him she'll never see him again.

Your B stories, or secondary plots, develop further here, too—whether they're secondary love stories, best friend subplots, red herrings, or the paperboy wanting his two dollars. In *The Princess Bride*, the main story is about Wesley trying to rescue Princess Buttercup, but the B story is Inigo Montoya and his hunt for the six-fingered man who killed his father. While the main story is the focus, and the B stories support it, readers are invested in both stories and want to see how they both turn out. So, it's important to keep all the threads moving along, supporting the main plot, and creating a rich story, which makes plotting imperative to writing a solid novel.

In *The Princess Bride*, Inigo Montoya ends up finding and killing the six-fingered man. In *The Hunger Games*, the B story is Katniss and Peeta's romance. In *The Holiday*, the B story is Kate Winslet's adorable relationship with the old man next door who becomes her only friend in LA. No matter how many subplots you have, they must reach a resolution in the end. That doesn't mean they have to resolve happily, but they must resolve in one way or another. If you introduce a brother whose chronic illness forces the main character to go home for a visit just so you can get your main character there, you'd better resolve the brother's illness. Don't just leave him hanging.

The Choice

The choice the character makes in response to the inciting incident is the beginning of Act II. It can be to face it head on, or to run from it, but the journey has started, and the character must face the consequences of their decision. This is where you show what kind of person your character is. It's important at this point that the character remains consistent with the type of person you initially show them to be. If you make your character out to be brave and heroic, you can't have them run and hide later in the story unless there is good reason for it. Conversely, if they are timid or untrustworthy at the start, no one will believe it if they suddenly become a pillar of strength unless you show a reason for this dramatic transformation—which might be the whole reason for the story. Once the character makes their first choice, there will be a number of choices they must make until they hit the crisis, and ultimately, the climax, of the story.

Obstacles and relief and more obstacles

These are the main plot points of the story. Obstacles are a series of challenges that your character must face in order to overcome the major issue that prevents them from obtaining their goal, whether that goal is to get the love interest, cure the disease, save the world, find the treasure, or to defeat evil. Obstacles can come in the form of almost anything as long as they stand in the way of the character's primary desire.

This is where much of the true art of storytelling comes in. Up until now, you have set the stage and provided the jumping off point and, yes, you have used quite a bit of imagination, but this is where strategic thinking comes in. At some point during all this setup and creation of a reason for the story, you need to have an inkling of how the story will turn out. Maybe you don't have the specific details, but you know something about the ending. Your character, as the seeker, will find something, be it redemption, love, truth, peace, validation, continued life, etc. Whatever it is, you know they will get it—so, Act II is the place when you'll make it interesting for the character and for the reader. Remember that every obstacle and decision made during this part should propel the story forward. This is not the place to bring up major issues that are not relevant to the plot. If something happens here, you must connect it to the story. It's not enough to be interesting. It must provide momentum toward the final goal.

In *The Wizard of Oz*, Dorothy needs intelligence, compassion, and courage to defeat the Wizard, so she meets the Scarecrow, the Tin Woodsman, and the Cowardly Lion, whom she needs when she gets to Emerald City. She doesn't need beauty, wealth, or dexterity, so L. Frank Baum didn't make her meet a movie star, a billionaire, and a circus performer. They would have just detracted from the story.

Obstacles are also used to show the characters' qualities. They might prove that your main character is the only one in the universe capable of solving the central conflict of the story. A challenge will reveal their true strength or weakness. Your character might appear incapable of accomplishing the task, but something might change the direction of the story entirely, and the main character becomes the perfect person to do it. Take, for instance, *Forrest Gump* when, time after time, he was able to do something no one ever thought he could. Come on! Who would have predicted he could play ping pong the way he did? This wasn't just a fun detail. Forrest Gump's endorsement of a ping pong paddle gave him the money to start his shrimping business in memory of Bubba.

And finally, and maybe most importantly, obstacles should build the tension by making the reader believe that the character may fail. In most stories, the tension will ebb and flow, as well, so the reader doesn't know what to expect. Although, in a horror story, it might just build and build until the reader is so tightly strung that the slightest thing will make them jump. We're talking to you, Stephen King!

Absolute disaster

Finally, to close out Act II, the final obstacle is presented as the absolute disaster. When it feels like it can't get any more dire. The sky is about to fall, and it seems that nothing can be done to clear the final challenge. Your character is certain to fail. This is the event that builds up to the climax, which begins Act III.

Act III: The Climax and the Falling action

The Climax

The climax occurs just as you move into Act III. It's the moment of truth. There's a reason this is called the climax—everyone is holding their breath because they don't think they can handle it for another moment, and then BOOM! The main character says, "I can't live without you." It's Ripley fighting the alien queen in *Alien*. It's the detective in *The Usual Suspects* gazing around his office as he realizes Keyser Soze just made up his entire story. It's Richard Gere's character marching back into the factory in *An Officer and a Gentleman* and picking up Debra Winger's character to carry her off to her new life. It's what you've been building up to throughout your entire story, and you cannot let your reader down at this point. They're counting on you.

The Falling Action

Just as it sounds, the falling action consists of the events that bring the reader down from the dizzying heights you've taken them to. They are emotionally vulnerable and need gentle hands to bring them back to a safe place. In essence, the remainder of the book is the falling action, which contains the following:

Processing and Dénouement

The characters integrate what they have gained and learned, and transform themselves in a way that enhances their new lives. They will never be the same again. It's usually the moment when the detective wraps up how he figured things out. It's your coldhearted main character realizing where they've gone wrong for so long. It's Harry Potter sitting in Dumbledore's office, parsing out why things went the way they did. A lot of processing takes place in Act III. Each subplot in the story gets tied up here if they haven't already been closed.

This is also when the writer looks back and makes sure each character had an active role in moving the story forward. Occasionally, an incredibly interesting character makes an appearance, and the writer falls in love with them, but they just aren't critical to the story development. The sometimes sad reality is that if the character doesn't reveal something to make the story move forward, you should remove the character. Just as with obstacles, it isn't enough to be an interesting character—they must be instrumental to propelling the story forward.

> **Pro Tip:** If you have a supporting character who doesn't substantially support the story, but one or more of their actions are needed to propel the plot forward, you can rewrite their contribution via the actions of a different, more substantial character. Additionally, if you have more than one side character with minimal contributions, you can rewrite both characters into a single substantial character.

Last Revelations

Sometimes this can be a surprise twist just before The End or the credits roll, and sometimes it's part of tying up the loose strings. Stories like *American Psycho*, *The Sixth Sense*, and *Fight Club* come to mind. When you think the main plot is tied up, but then BAMMO! A revelation sizzles your mind.

And that is Act III. It's likely to be your shortest section. In some romances, the book might end right after the climax.

To epilogue or not to epilogue

First of all, what is an epilogue? An epilogue is a final section at the end of a book that shows the reader the fates of the characters in the story. It's usually much shorter than a chapter and is very much to the point. A good example of an epilogue is the final bit at the very end of the final *Harry Potter* book, which shows the kids as grown-ups with children of their own. After such a perilous stretch in which Harry Potter and his friends are almost killed several times, it is a much-appreciated glimpse into the future showing that they are all safe and sound and living normal lives after defeating He Who Shall Not Be Named. Well, they live as normal lives as wizards usually live.

Occasionally, epilogues are used to make way for a sequel or a series, although they are not required for them.

An epilogue should look forward, not look back. By this, we mean it shouldn't be used to close out plot points, provide additional details of the story, or explain the moral of the story. Those should have been accomplished in the story.

And that, Dear Writer, is Plotting and Outlining.

Now, to tie it all up…

You can see why we put plotting and outlining in the same chapter. One naturally informs the other. Although there are various plot structures, they all follow a similar flow that includes setup, rising action, a climax, and finally, the falling action. Readers are used to this and will be uncomfortable, or even upset, if the story does not progress the way they are accustomed to. This means that you need to put some forethought into your story to ensure the structure unfolds smoothly. Outlining is a good way of accomplishing this and keeping the writer on track.

Some people prefer to create a formal outline of major plot

points prior to starting on their story to give themselves a map to work from. The outline doesn't have to be complex; it can be as simple as a list of bullet points arranged in a logical order. Other people can do this in their heads, but an outline is still involved, even if it isn't written out. Once the major plot points are mapped out, you have enough of an outline to start writing.

As you develop the plot and outline, your characters will almost certainly start to emerge and take shape. Likewise, as you're writing about your characters, you may learn something that affects your plot. Because of this, we think it's best to plan before writing so you can avoid unexpected snags in the story that may take extra time to unsnarl or, worse, cause you to become frustrated and/or unmotivated to continue writing.

And finally...

> **Pro Tip:** If you run into a problem with your story or find yourself with writer's block, pausing to write or update your outline may help you figure out the problem or kick-start your creativity.

See it in Action: *The Shadow Hunters*

We've taken what we've discussed in this chapter and created the beginning of an outline for a story we're calling *The Shadow Hunters*. The inspiration for this story came from an idea about a young woman who must find and return an amulet to its rightful empress in order to restore peace to an empire.

Act I: *The Beginning*

Opening scene*:

*Not all stories have an opening scene, but we decided to use one here because we are writing a frame narrative (i.e., a story within a story), and we have to orient the reader.

An elderly person sits at a campfire talking to a group of children. (The reader doesn't know this, but it is the Shadow Hunter, Eldric, who comes into the book later.) They tell the children that it's important to hear this story because their world was once at war, and it was saved because of one woman.

It starts like this: Once upon a time, a young woman named Kyrie [figure out last name*] was chosen to sacrifice herself to save the world.

*Notice the note regarding the character's last name. We didn't want our process to get bogged down in small details. When making the outline, be careful to not spend too much time fussing about names, settings, and other small details. These can drag you down and keep you from finishing your outline. Instead, make a note in some way, as we did here, and move on, knowing you can always come back to it later.

The setup:

Introduce your main character and give the reader a hint of trouble in their real world. Bring in elements of setting.

Kyrie and her parents are living in tents in the forest of Alnight. The world is at war, royalty has been deposed, and factions are fighting. An overlord (evil dictator) sits on the throne at Castle Gorn. People are starving; people are being killed for minor offenses. Kyrie and her parents belong to a rebel faction that seeks to restore the benevolent monarchy and bring peace back to the empire ~~kingdom~~*. The theme is something along the lines of good triumphs over evil, as well as the main character discovers who they really are.

*In the first draft of our outline, we had the power structure as a kingdom, but since it is under matriarchal rule, we decided to change to an empire. Note that we didn't let this stop us from plotting. We came back to it once we started writing.

The inciting incident:

What forces your character to take their journey?

Kyrie's mother takes her aside and tells her they are the true rulers of this land. Tells her the family's magic amulet was stolen by a traitor to the throne, driving the world into war and forcing Kyrie's family into hiding. Kyrie's parents tell her she must travel across the land, disguise herself as a member of one of the rival factions, and steal the amulet back.

It has to be her because, in order for the family to regain power, they must be the ones to defeat the current ruler.

The meet cute (for romances):

The moment the two main characters first meet. In a non-romance, this can still happen. Perhaps the main character meets the antagonist or a mentor figure.

Kyrie and her best friend, ~~Willow~~ Soteria*, talk about the quest—establish this relationship. There will probably be a romance as a sub-plot but we're not sure who the romance will be with.**

*We decided to switch to Soteria after discussing the popularity of the name Willow as a sidekick in fantasy books. We really like it but wanted to use a more unique name. By the way, you will see a few notes like this in our *See it in Action* sections, because we want to show you just how the real writing process progresses. The idea is to keep going and annotate as you go to remind yourself why you've done certain things because, believe us, you will read some of the stuff you write and see changes you made and have no recollection of ever doing it.

**Notice this section isn't fully fleshed out. We weren't sure of all the details of this relationship except that we want ~~Willow~~ Soteria to go on the quest with Kyrie. So we put a short note here, knowing we may spark our creativity when we start writing.

The debate/second thoughts:

The main character debates whether they can succeed at their goal and thinks about the consequences. They have doubts. They may start seeing things they really love about their current situation and may not want to jeopardize it.

Kyrie isn't sure she will be successful at retrieving the amulet, she doesn't want to leave her village, nor does she believe in fighting. She's a pacifist. On the other hand, she loves her parents and wants to help them.

Act II: The Middle:

The choice:

The main character makes a decision, and the reader starts to learn what price the main character may have to pay to take this journey.

Kyrie and ~~Willow~~ Soteria decide to take a chance and make the journey. They visit an elder, who gives them maps of the land for their quest. A village seer, Kassandra the Eye, sees them packing to go and says, "One of you will not return from this journey."*

*Here, we'll make sure to drop some hints about the relationship between Kyrie and the seer. Perhaps the seer is a midwife who delivered Kyrie; perhaps Kassandra had other obligations in the empire long before she took the path of becoming a seer. Whatever it is, we know we have to establish a connection here because the seer will be aiding Kyrie later in the story, and we want the reader to find that believable.

Side characters:

Develop side characters. Introduce or further develop subplots.

Kyrie's parents work in the background to find out who the traitor is. They think Kyrie's uncle has been killed during the coup, but really, he is the betrayer and is living the high life in the castle with the new dictator. A cat seems to follow them, mysteriously appears, and disappears, often giving info that will help them.

Obstacles:

What happens to keep the main character from reaching their goal? (It's good to have a brief triumph over this obstacle. It won't last.)

Kyrie and best friend run into the Shadow Hunters.*

*Note we need more development here. Rather than stop to figure out these details because we aren't yet sure what's going to happen in this part of the story, we'll leave this as a placeholder and move on.

Relief:

A point in the story when everything seems to be going well. The main character starts to feel confident. They've won a small victory and feel very positive about what they have accomplished so far.

Somehow, Kyrie and ~~Willow~~ Soteria evade the Shadow Hunters. [Need to figure this out—is there a fight? Do they use magic? Eldric has to be involved somehow. We need to maintain a feeling that Eldric could be either a good person or an adversary.]*

*Notice we didn't add too much detail here before we started writing the manuscript. There are situations that happen to the characters, and a lot of character development needs to occur, but we want to see how the story progresses as we write. And as we write, we will fill in the outline to keep track of what occurs in the story so we can refer to it as we go. You can see what we ultimately came up with in Appendix 1—The Planning of *The Shadow Hunters*.

More obstacles:

After the first obstacle, the main character starts to feel they have a plan. This obstacle wrecks that plan and raises the stakes.

Kyrie and ~~Willow~~ Soteria sense they are being tracked, and they are—by Eldric, who knows they should capture them or possibly worse, but is reluctant to carry out the even worse option. The cat keeps Eldric at bay.

Kyrie and ~~Willow~~ Soteria run out of food. Eldric wants to help them but battles their allegiance. Eldric knows they will have to turn back or possibly die and is at war with their loyalty to the evil dictator.

The harsh terrain and creatures they encounter challenge the group. Finally, dragons attack them. The group has to work together to survive. A wary truce. Kyrie also finds she has magic she was unaware of.

There is a final barrier before Kyrie and ~~Willow~~ Soteria can get into the castle. Eldric shows them how to overcome it, creating trust but not complete trust.

Absolute disaster:

This is the biggest obstacle, the moment when the main character loses everything they've worked for to this moment. It's the obstacle that makes your main character think the battle will never be won and all is over. Don't forget to give your main character some time to hate their life right now. Everything is lost (they think), and they'll never win. They deserve to have some time to wallow.

~~Willow~~ Soteria is killed (by Uncle, betrayer). OH! Kyrie and her parents thought Uncle was dead, but Kyrie and best friend find him in the castle serving with the evil overlord. Kyrie escapes and heads to the woods without the amulet, giving up on her quest. The cat appears and she decides she has to try again. [Where is Eldric?]

Act III: The End

Climax:

The moment of truth. It's the gut punch of the plot where the main character either gets everything they want or realizes they're never going to get it. It's the moment the reader has been waiting for.

Kyrie fights the uncle and the evil dictator—she's about to lose, but the cat shows up and claws Uncle's eyes out. He stumbles to the back of the room and falls out the castle tower window, dying on the ground below. The evil dictator manages to get hold of Kyrie and puts his hands around her neck to strangle her. Kyrie rips the amulet from his neck and throws it to the cat and says, "Get this to my parents."

Eldric, changing allegiance because of their love (or is it allegiance?) for Kyrie, rushes in and chops off the dictator's head, as the dictator is no longer protected by the amulet. This cements Eldric's change of allegiance from the dictator to Kyrie.

Falling action:

This allows you to wrap up any B stories and subplots. Maybe a little obstacle comes in here, but it's resolved easily. Falling action brings the reader down from the intensity of the rising action and climax.

Kyrie and Eldric go back to the tent village.

Kyrie gives the amulet to her mother.

Processing:

The characters get to talk about what happened. This is the chance to tie up loose ends.

Why did the uncle go bad?

Why did Eldric become a Shadow Hunter?

What becomes of Eldric's love for Kyrie?

Denouement:

The end. The characters live happily ever after, or they don't. Everything is completely wrapped up, unless it's a sequel, in which case, you might leave a dangling tidbit.

The empire improves under the empress's reinstatement. Kyrie learns how to use her powers and goes into training to become her mother's successor.

How's that for an example, huh? As you can see, it isn't a fully detailed synopsis of the story, but it is a good outline to get started with, containing the progression of plot elements, a handful of plot points, and at least a couple of subplots. We also have an idea of the theme. It's a good place to start and guarantees us a map to keep us going, while still allowing us a lot of opportunity to remain creative. And, hey, if we naturally go in a direction we didn't plan on, we can reassess at any time and change the outline to accommodate the new ideas.

Our creative brains are exploding with ideas now.

Summary

There's a *lot* of information in this chapter, and if you're new to plotting, it may seem a little overwhelming. It's okay to go back and read it again. Take some time with the short activity in the beginning of the chapter where we give you a couple of movie trailers to watch to help you see how the seven basic plot points:

1. Setup

2. Inciting incident

3. Goals/desires

4. Opponent

5. Rising action

6. Climax

7. Resolution

This should ease you into the idea of plotting and outlining.

Remember, you don't have to do it this way. Like any other process, you'll find what works best for you, and that may change as you move through your writing journey, learning and becoming a stronger writer with every story. The information in this chapter is meant to help you find your way through the basics of plotting your novel.

Remember, ultimately the plot and structure of your novel are simply the skeleton holding the body up.

Now you get to go add some flesh and blood to it!

Frequently asked questions

Can I start writing even if I haven't finished my outline?

Sure! Sometimes it's almost impossible to hold back on

starting to write when an idea is just clamoring to be expressed. We do recommend frequently coming back to the outline as you continue writing so you can see the progression of the plot structure and to make sure it is still on track with your planning. If something changes along the way and it makes sense to continue with it, you can always update your outline with the new information. We've found that it's helpful to continue to add the new plot points to the outline even if you've already written the scenes, so you can refer to them as you move through the story. It may help keep you on track, and it can provide you with a map if you feel like you've gotten lost at any point.

What if I'm still feeling overwhelmed and unsure how to start?

If you still find this all way too much, take a deep breath. Take a break. Maybe get a snack or go for a walk. When you come back to your computer, ask yourself who your main character is, what she wants in life, and what stands in the way.

Got it? Great, you've taken your first step in plotting!

What if I've read all of this, and I still can't figure out how to plot?

Try using the Story Arc worksheet in Appendix 3, where we have several worksheets! It will guide you through step by step.

What if I've read all of this and still don't want to do an outline of my plot?

Some people are just not plotters, and that's okay. Don't force yourself to do something that doesn't help you. By reading this, you're already more knowledgeable than you were before, so that's something. And if you ever find yourself having a hard time with a story you've written, where something just doesn't seem to work, you can come back to this chapter and do an outline after the fact. It may help you to deconstruct the story and identify where you missed a piece of the structure.

Recommended Resources

If you need more plotting instruction, a few great books we recommend are:

- *Save the Cat! The Last Book on Screenwriting You'll Ever Need* by Blake Snyder, Michael Wiese Productions, 2005 (Also, the *Save the Cat!* website is a valuable resource—https://savethecat.com)

- *Romancing the Beat: Story Structure for Romance Novels* by Gwen Hayes, Gwen Hayes, 2016

- *Structuring Your Novel: Essential Keys for Writing an Outstanding Story* by K.M. Weiland, PenForASword Publishing, 2013

Discussion Time

Finnian and Kimberly talk about how they evolved their plotting processes.

Plotting and Outlining Pt 1: https://youtu.be/ WoxC3soVEQM

Plotting and Outlining Pt 2: https://youtu.be/ NpvENPNRTIY

Try it out

For all writers:

Without doing any plotting or outlining, write a 200-word short story using one of the writing prompts we've provided in the appendix.

Now, using what we've discussed in this chapter, take a second writing prompt, plot the simple story arc and basic outline, and write a 200-word short story. (Your outline may end up being longer than the story you end up with.)

Point of View

Literary Point of View—The vantage point from which the narrator is telling the story. The main components of this are who is telling the story, what information they have access to, and to whom they are telling the story.

Places are never just places in a piece of writing. If they are, the author has failed. Setting is not inert. It is activated by point of view. — **Carmen Maria Machado**

Introduction

In the simplest terms, point of view is how your readers get to experience your story. It's the narrator of the story, the person who is telling what to whom. Among other things, it sets the tone and pacing, allows the reader insight into the characters, and—depending on which point of view you intend to use—it determines the degree of connection they will have with the characters in your book.

Selecting the right POV for your story is important for many reasons, but we believe the top three are: access to information needed to keep the story flowing; depth of connection the reader has with the story; and it keeps the reader from getting confused or lost. We'll go into more detail about these reasons and more as we dive deeper into this concept.

In addition, this chapter will go over the various points of view at your disposal, provide examples, talk about the benefits and limitations of each, and help guide your decision about which point of view will work best for your story.

Ready? Let's go!

What It's All About

It's common for a new writer to not give much thought about point of view when they begin writing their first story. Their inclination is to just start throwing down words to get the story going. We totally get it. A new story is an idea and, to a creative mind, the fleshing out of that new idea consists of letting *it* tell *you* how it will be told.

So, they just start writing.

> *The bartender glanced up at Kyrie as she walked into the bar. In the dim light, his dark eyes showed disdain as she slid into a seat. Kyrie caught her breath, wondering if he knew about the amulet. She'd been careful, but the Shadow Hunters were clever, and they were everywhere. Could he be one? She wanted to run, but she needed to find out what he*

knew. The fire dagger strapped to her waist gave her courage, but it would do nothing against an antimatter propulsion gun.

First drafts are all about just getting the story down on the page, right? We believe in writing it out and making it shine in rewrites. So, that's what we did here. We just got the basics of the scene down on paper so we can continue to add to it as the story evolves in our mind.

Now, let's talk about it in terms of point of view.

We don't know much about this story from this short paragraph, but we do know that Kyrie seems to be a main character and she knows something about an amulet. Furthermore, she's frightened by the bartender, who knows something she needs to know, but he doesn't seem very approachable. In fact, she is concerned that he might be a Shadow Hunter, someone she needs to avoid.

As readers, we're already hooked. As writers, we have a lot of work to do.

Going forward, a reader will expect to learn more about Kyrie and the bartender and how they factor into the story. The story starts with her, but maybe Kyrie isn't a main character. Maybe she's just a minor character and the author plans to kill her off in the bar when the bartender discovers *she* has the information *he* needs. Maybe the main character is a person watching from a booth in the corner, waiting to overhear Kyrie and the bartender's conversation, and the fact that we wrote the first scene in limited third person (third person through Kyrie's point of view), it just made it difficult to tell the rest of the story from the real main character's point of view.

So many possibilities, especially since we just wrote the first scene without knowing about the rest of the story. If Kyrie doesn't turn out to be the main character, or if other characters come up in the story who have information that Kyrie doesn't have access to, we may find it difficult to proceed at certain points of the story. It can be done, but if the writer knows more about the story from the start, it will make it less likely that they will run into trouble later on.

In order to answer all the reader's questions and to tell the story in the most effective way, we have to choose the right narrator for the story. The best choice will always be the one that provides the most effective way to impart the details of the story to the reader. If Kyrie gets killed off, she can't carry the story beyond the point where the murder takes place, unless she's a ghost who continues to tell the story after the living character gets killed off. If the bartender or another character is telling the story, how do they know what she's wondering and feeling? If a narrator who knows all things at all times, otherwise known as an omniscient narrator, is telling the story, there's almost an unlimited wealth of knowledge at their disposal. But in order to maintain tension throughout the story and to give the reader a sense of connection, the writer must decide how much information to impart at what time and maintain a consistency of depth, so the reader doesn't feel manipulated.

Who's going to possess this knowledge? Will it be the main character? Will it be the bartender? Will it be another character who is privy to all the information needed to effectively tell the story? Maybe it's a character that is never even named in the story, just some person who happens to be there like some invisible spy, keeping track of everything going on—our omniscient character.

In general terms, there are three points of view:

First person—*told from the "I" perspective.*

Example: I sat down, and the bartender looked at me.

Second person—*told from the "you" perspective.*

Example: You sat down, and the bartender looked at you.

Third person—*told from an "other" perspective.*

Example: They (or he, or she) sat down, and the bartender looked at them (or him, or she).

We'll go into much deeper detail on all three perspectives later in the chapter.

Pro Tip: When discussing point of view, it is beneficial to know the term **viewpoint character**. The viewpoint character is the guide through part or all of the story, providing information that they have that will give the reader a sense of what the story is about. Many times, the viewpoint character is the main character, or the protagonist; other times it is an all-knowing entity, otherwise known as an omniscient narrator; and still other times, it may be multiple characters. The idea is that the story is told from the perspective of a single entity at any given time, which gives the reader a sense of orientation in the story. Regardless of who the viewpoint character is, it is a good thing to refrain from moving from one narrator to another without very clear communication to the reader that you are doing so. The reader's connection to your story is delicate and can be broken very easily, and not being clear on who is telling the story is one common way to break that connection.

Based on the paragraph we've written, it already appears that the story will probably be best told from a third person perspective. There are no "I" or "me" words to show it's being told in first person, and there are no "you" words indicating it is in second person. However, we could go back and change to either of those points of view if the story seems to merit one of them. Third person is a very popular point of view in sci-fi/fantasy novels, so that might make sense for this story.

If you're a plotter, which we talk about in much greater detail in the previous chapter on Plot and Outline, you'll have planned the story out, and it will be easier to know which character will have the needed information at the right times, making them the best for telling the story. If you're not a major plotter and you prefer to create the story as you go along, you may not even know all the characters in the story yet. Either way is fine. Each writer has their own process. But if you're a pantser, you'll probably just have to pick one point of view and go with it. Chances are you'll make the point of view you chose work as you go along, but there is also a chance that you'll find, as the story takes more shape, that another point of view will work better. Then you'll have to revise the story at a later date to incorporate the new point of view into the sections you wrote before you changed it.

The point is, you may be able to decide the perfect point of view before you even start, or you may not settle on the best point of view until you've written a good portion of your story. But, hey, that's what first drafts are for. You can clean it up during revisions.

The main thing to take from this discussion is that you want to prevent inconsistent POV and avoid unnecessarily changing points of view, which are a couple of the most common errors emerging writers make—and, let's be honest, some established writers, as well.

Like most writing rules, though, once you've mastered them, you can play with them, even break them, if the story supports it. We've said before: you can do anything you want to as long as you know why you're doing it and can find a solid way of pulling it off. In the meantime, we'll tell you about the different points of view, show you what they look like, and give some ideas on how to use them.

In this chapter, we're going to talk about the following points of view:

First person

Second person

Third person—as well as the different types of third person:

Third person limited

Third person objective

Third person omniscient

First Person

This is the perspective using *I*, *me*, and sometimes *we* if first person collective is being used. This point of view is written as if the character is describing the events as they happened, are happening, or will happen to themselves.

> *The bartender glanced up as I walked into the bar. In the soft light, his dark eyes looked almost black, and disdain crawled across his face as I slid into a seat. My breath caught in my throat. Did he know I carried the amulet? I'd been careful to cover my tracks, but the Shadow Hunters were clever, and they were everywhere. He could be one. A war between a desire to run and a desire to find out what he knew played in my head. The fire dagger at my waist was the only reason I didn't turn around right away. Although, if he was a Shadow Hunter, the antimatter propulsion gun he carried would make my knife as effective as a drained yak bladder.*

Some naysayers call first person an amateur's point of view. That simply isn't true. Perhaps it's because some people find first person easiest to write, leading them to believe that easy somehow equates to immature. Personally, we love first person point of view. It gives a work a sense of immediacy that other points of view can't provide.

Some truly stellar books are written in first person. If you want to see great examples of this point of view, read *Never Let Me Go* by Kazuo Ishiguro or *Kindred* by Octavia Butler.

First person has some incredible benefits. First, your reader will be intimately involved with your main character, knowing everything they think, sense, and do. This works well with a beloved character or someone easily relatable. Alternatively, it may not work as well with an unsympathetic or dull character, because it can be hard for the reader to stay engaged with a person who has nothing on their mind, or to get up and personal with the inner thoughts of a psychopath. But if the character is interesting and you allow the reader into their head, it can create a compelling narrative. Just know that if your character isn't likable, they must be complex and entertaining. No one wants to read two hundred pages of some dullard whining about their boring life or about a criminal who only has bloodlust on their mind.

First person allows the reader to feel more deeply as if they are experiencing the story as they read it. Perhaps that's why it's so popular in YA novels. The ability to live inside the main character's head makes the character feel like a friend.

On the flip side, first person has limitations.

Primarily, the reader will only ever get to see things from one person's viewpoint. That means the readers don't know anything the character doesn't know or what goes on when the character isn't there. Things that happen outside of the character's presence, such as while the reader is asleep or when they are across town from the event, need to be relayed to the character in some fashion so they can be presented to the reader. In this way, the reader can only see the character react to the things revealed to them after the fact.

Pro Tip: Show, don't tell. This bit of advice is sometimes referred to as the Golden Rule of writing. Show, don't tell is a writing technique that relies more on sensory description rather than explanation, also known as expository writing, to tell a story. In this way a writer is *showing* the reader the scene rather than *telling* them about it. It allows the reader to immerse themselves in the writing, which, to many, is a better reading experience.

Another pitfall of first person POV is that it can be easy to fall into telling, rather than showing. A writer can slip into describing what the character is thinking and feeling— because the writer knows it all, right? But remember, the reader will be more immersed in the story if they can *see* the character shivering in the snow or getting goose bumps when someone touches them in just the right way.

What sounds better?

> *It was cold as I made my way through the scary, abandoned graveyard. It felt inhospitable. I wanted to run away, but I stayed on the path. I couldn't stop now. The Shadow Hunters were close behind.*

Or...

Goose bumps rose on my arms, and it wasn't just because of the gravestones on either side of the overgrown path. The names etched into the stone were worn and illegible, the slabs of granite sinking into the damp earth. Inhospitable figures seemed to lurk behind them, ready to grab me. I fought the urge to run back the way I came, but my destination was up ahead, and I couldn't stop now, not with the Shadow Hunters breathing down my neck.

As you can see, first person point of view puts you, the reader, in the story, as if you are walking through the graveyard, as if your heartbeat is thumping through your veins.

One advantage of first-person point of view is the ease with which you can use an unreliable narrator. An example of this is experienced in the novel *The Curious Incident of the Dog in the Night-Time* by Mark Haddon, where a fifteen-year-old boy, who is implied in the book to be on the autism spectrum, tells the story.

Try it yourself

For all writers:

It's the first day of kindergarten, and the children are entering their new classroom for the first time.

Write it from the point of view of the:

- Kindergartener

- Teacher

- School janitor

A Note about First Person Collective

While we're talking about first person, we wanted to expand on a subset of first person called first person collective, which we briefly mentioned above. A classic example of this point of view is in the William Faulkner short story, *A Rose for Emily*. First person collective is unusual in that the narrator is a group of people, so instead of using I, the author uses "we" as the characters' narrative pronoun.

> *When Miss Emily Grierson died, our whole town went to her funeral: the men through a sort of respectful affection for a fallen monument, the women mostly out of curiosity to see the inside of her house, which no one save an old man-servant—a combined gardener and cook—had seen in at least ten years. – William Faulkner, A Rose for Emily.*

The freedom of first-person collective is that it gives the author a chance to jump from character to character, and it allows the reader insight into things they wouldn't necessarily know. We can follow the sheriff into the main character's house, or we can gossip with the townsfolk. We can participate in the funeral, or we can be part of the gruesome discovery at the end of the story.

In *It Was an Affair* by Finnian Burnett in the anthology, *Conference Call*, we're part of the group, watching a love story develop between the two main characters.

> *We stood next to them at the lunch buffet, watching*

as they carefully didn't touch. Their bodies seemed to crane toward each other until they caught themselves and rearranged the space between them to an appropriate distance. We could feel the pull as they found seats next to each other at a table. They made conversation with the others, but their arms touched, and they bumped hands as they ate.

In this example, notice the narrators are telling the story, but the action is taking place between the two lovers.

If you're interested in reading a book written in this point of view, check out *The Weird Sisters* by Eleanor Brown. Notice how the author moves deftly between the collective narrator and the third person.

Try It Yourself

If you're interested in trying this point of view for yourself, start out thinking of the story you want to tell, and then ask yourself who would be watching the story unfold. That group is your collective narrator.

Or use one of the following prompts:

- The whole town knew Jack had killed Betty, but we didn't know what to do about it.

- We watched Sally struggle down the street with a baby and eight bags of groceries, but we didn't step up to help.

- The three of us grew up hating our parents.

Second Person

The bartender glanced up as you walked into the bar. In the soft light, his dark eyes looked almost black, and disdain crawled across his face as you slid into a seat. Your breath caught in your throat. Did he know you carried the amulet? You'd been careful to cover your tracks, but the Shadow Hunters were clever, and they were everywhere. He could have been one. A war between a desire to run and a desire to find out what he knew played in your head. You rested your hand on the fire dagger at your waist, knowing it would be no match for the antimatter propulsion gun he was carrying if he was, indeed, a Shadow Hunter.

Second person is an excellent POV for short pieces, especially super short pieces like flash and micro fiction, although it can feel somewhat removed, less intimate, than first person. It can be a great point of view to practice writing something that you're afraid to write. The distance puts a psychological safety barrier between the author and the subject matter, making it easier to tackle difficult subjects. However, second person can be hard to sustain for an entire novel, though some have done it. An example of this is *Half-Asleep in Frog Pajamas* by Tom Robbins. Remember the *Choose Your Own Adventure* children's books that were so popular in the 80s and early 90s? Those were all written in second person.

This point of view can be difficult to master, but it's such a fun exercise. And it's unusual—if you can master it, it may make your work stand out to an editor. Conversely, an editor who is bothered by second person might toss your story because they don't like the POV, so it's good to know your audience before committing to something that may put some readers off.

We recommend experimenting with second person point of view because it's unusual, and sometimes, slipping into another point of view can help loosen up the creative muscles if you're feeling stuck.

Try It Yourself

If you want to practice this point of view without committing to it, try taking a short story you've already written in first person and switching it to second person, just to see how it feels.

Or try one of the following prompts:

- You walk into a bar in Texas, and...

- You were fifteen the first time you saw someone die.

- The roll of thunder drowns out your voice as you scream at your sister, trying to get her attention.

Third Person Limited

In third person limited, the narrator is in one person's mind, telling the story from their perspective. It isn't the actual character telling the story, which is first person, but the narrator has access to the thoughts and experiences of the character.

The bartender glanced up as Kyrie walked into the bar. In the soft light, his dark eyes looked almost black, and disdain crawled across his face as she slid into a seat. Her breath caught in her throat. She focused on keeping her face impassive, not giving into the fear. Did he know she had the amulet, or was he just a jerk in general? She'd been careful to cover her tracks, but the Shadow Hunters were clever, and they were everywhere. One had been following her for weeks before she finally managed to shake him off in the last town. The bartender could be one. She forced herself to meet his gaze as a war between a desire to run and a desire to find out the truth raged in her head.

It's easy to think of this as all-knowing, or omniscient, but since it is limited to the one character, it really isn't.

We'll go into more detail about third person omniscient a little later, but the easiest way to understand the difference between third person limited and omniscient is this: In omniscient, the narrator is a separate entity who knows all the history, background, setting details, and character's thoughts, feelings, motivations. The omniscient narrator is not your protagonist—it's someone else altogether. In third person limited, the narrator is in one person's head in a chapter or a given scene—Kyrie's head in the above scene. Since you're only reading from Kyrie's point of view, you have to ensure she's not privy to information she wouldn't know.

As you can see, this limited point of view does not show what the other characters are thinking or experiencing except from the viewpoint character in this case, Kyrie. Kyrie can see disdain on his face, but she doesn't know what is causing it, or if that's just the way his face always looks.

A benefit of using third person limited is that it allows the writer to give the reader close contact with one character's thoughts and feelings. That makes this one of the best points of view, alongside first person, to use in close distance or up-close storytelling, which are ways to create intimacy or immediacy in a story. It's also easier to maintain suspense because there are things your protagonist/narrator can't know until they are specifically shown by another character or through the character experiencing it. Also, it is a great point of view in which to introduce an unreliable narrator, instead of relying on a first-person point of view or, less likely, third person omniscient.

Pro Tip: We've mentioned **unreliable narrators** a couple of times now, so it might be time to provide a little more information about them. An unreliable narrator is just what it sounds like, a narrator who cannot be relied upon to present accurate details in the telling of a story. Oftentimes, the unreliable narrator is a great plot tool that can be called upon to keep the reader guessing, or sometimes to introduce a twist in the story, creating tension and more interest in the story.

Sometimes, the author lets the reader know upfront when the narrator is unreliable so the reader knows they can't believe everything told to them. The character Scout in *To Kill a Mockingbird* is an example of one such unreliable narrator because the reader knows from the beginning that she is too young to understand the very adult things she is talking about. Other times, it is only in hindsight that the reader finds that the narrator has been unreliable all along. A good example of this is *The Girl on the Train* by Paula Hawkins in which the main character, Rachel Watson, is found to be an alcoholic and thus has been manipulated to believe certain things that may or may not be true.

We mention above that third person limited is the least risky POV in which to introduce an unreliable narrator because it's easy to introduce doubt about the narrator through their own personal limitations. In addition, remember when we noted earlier in the first person section that it is easy for a narrator to slip into expository writing in first person? Using sensory description will usually immerse a reader in such a way that they are able to suspend disbelief and accept an unreliable narrator more readily. Finally, because omniscient narrators are supposed to know everything, it is very rare to see an unreliable omniscient narrator, but it has been done and is almost always only accepted if the narrator is upfront about being unreliable. A couple of examples are Russian poet, Alexander Pushkin's *Eugene Onegin: A Novel in Verse*, where the narrator comes right out and says they are only interested in their own views and are not interested in consistency, and Russian author, Nikolai Gogol's *Dead Souls*, in which the narrator is outright in their sarcasm. In most other works, using an unreliable narrator in omniscient point of view would cause the reader to be pulled out of the story, wondering why the narrator didn't have access to credible information through other means, or worse, they might get angry about being led to believe one thing only to have it be another just because the author felt like messing with them. Thus, third person limited point of view provides the easiest method of using an unreliable narrator.

All of this is to say that third person limited POV is so popular because it gives the writer the intimacy of first person while still putting a bit of distance between the narrator and the reader. It allows the reader to slowly come to terms with the content of the story, building on their understanding, so they become fully immersed in what is happening.

So, those are the different facets of third person. Pretty fascinating, right?

Oh, wait.

Just to make sure we completely overwhelm you with all the points of view, there is also *third person limited, multiple character* point of view.

Yes, it's a thing, too. We didn't just make it up, and it's used when there is a group of characters who each tell a bit of the story, one at a time. This one comes close to third person omniscient, but it is still limited to only a focused group of characters. A good example of this is in Toni Morrison's novel, *Song of Solomon*. Morrison wrote the story from a third person point of view with individual characters relating what they are feeling and experiencing.

We almost forgot it because, sometimes, *third person limited, multiple character* is referred to as *limited omniscient*, and this wouldn't be wrong, as they essentially describe the same thing.

Try It Yourself

Two people are on their final full day of vacation, and they are sitting in a café in a foreign country. Write a scene in third person limited in which they are having an argument about what they want to do on their final day. Describe their gestures, their smiles, their words, and their thoughts. You will need to pick which character's point of view the narrator is telling the story from and be consistent in that point of view. If you want to take a shot at third person limited, multiple character, you can relate the scene again from the other character's point of view to provide even more information or a more interesting situation if the characters are seeing the situation in two very different ways, emotionally, intellectually, visually, etc.

Third Person Objective

Third person objective is when a story is written by a neutral narrator. It isn't a particularly intimate point of view, and it isn't widely used, especially among emerging writers. When you do see this point of view, it's usually being used to maintain a sense of mystery or a specific tone that complements the need for distance in a story. It's very difficult to build tension with this point of view, thus most writers avoid it. That said, we see people using third person objective by accident sometimes. If you have no insight into the character's feelings or inner thoughts, and you're simply reporting like an objective observer on their actions, you're in third person objective. And while this might work okay in a particular type of crime thriller, for the most part, readers want some hint of the main character's inner thoughts.

The bartender glanced up as the woman walked into the bar. In the soft light, his dark eyes looked almost black. A look of disdain crawled across his face. The woman slid onto a stool, holding a hand to her throat.

"I suppose you're going to ask me what I want to drink?" she said. Her hands drifted down to her pocket, and she seemed to grip something in it.

The bartender leaned across the bar. "What'll it be?"

Notice what we lose in this point of view compared to the earlier examples, particularly in a scene such as this. We don't know the woman is carrying an amulet and a dagger. We don't know the bartender might be one of the Shadow Hunters. And while this information may come out in the course of conversation, it can only be revealed by action or dialogue. We don't know what anyone is thinking or feeling.

The most famous example of this point of view is Ernest Hemingway's *Hills Like White Elephants*. In this story, Hemingway's narrator is an observer of a couple who are sitting at a nearby table. Through a clever use of dialogue and an understanding of words not necessarily meaning exactly what we think, Hemingway crafts an elegant, deep, and compelling story of two people unhappily coupled.

Though third person objective isn't necessarily a popular point of view, you may want to try it, whether to experiment with objectivity or simply for the fun of trying something new.

If you do decide to write in this POV, consider a couple of important points.

1. You don't know the character's names unless the narrator overhears them in dialogue.

2. The narrator is not omniscient—an omniscient narrator knows all the feelings of the characters and may even know what's going to happen in the future. The third person objective narrator doesn't know anything except what's right in front of them. That means we can only intuit what the characters are feeling by their dialogue and their body language.

3. It's a unique point of view that creates a very specific tone, which can fatigue a reader, so careful consideration should be given before you decide to use it.

Try It Yourself

Take a picture of two people and write their conversation as if you're overhearing it. You can describe their gestures, their smiles, their words—but not their thoughts. When you're revising, make sure to look for anything a watcher wouldn't know. The narrator can tell the reader that the main character sighed, but they can't say the main character sighed because she was frustrated.

Third Person Omniscient Point of View

Third person omniscient is, by far, the most open and versatile of points of view. Because it's so versatile there is almost infinite potential in the ways it can be used. This versatility makes it complicated to master. Yet, as complicated as it is, we love this POV.

If you've read *The Book Thief* by Markus Zusak, you'll know why. It's told in a deft and compelling manner that keeps the reader riveted to the page. A big reason for this is that the author chose Death to be the omniscient narrator. Death, as the narrator, is all-knowing and all-seeing but isn't a specific character in the book. Death's perspective allows the reader to know what each of the various characters are feeling, seeing, or thinking, without getting deep into any one character's psyche. While Zusak named Death as his omniscient narrator, many books using an omniscient narrator don't actually name the narrator. They portray their omniscient narrator more like the voice of a godlike entity, describing the events and details of the storyline as if they are privy to everything and anything—because they are. They know everything, past, present, and future.

Omniscient in this case doesn't mean God, though. It doesn't wield power over anything in the story or cause things to happen. It's a passive entity, simply relating events and information as a sagacious storyteller. The omniscient narrator is best understood as an individual with a single perspective, but one that has access to all information related to the story.

A classic example of an omniscient narrator can be experienced in the tale of *Beowulf*. This epic poem weaves in and out of the thoughts and histories of all the characters, letting the reader in on the motivations and back stories of many of them—even motivations the characters themselves are not aware of yet. This all-knowing narrator relates the history of the kingdom and the yearnings in the characters' hearts in the same breath as they describe Beowulf's epic deeds. It's a powerful means of storytelling, providing a richness of detail that engages a reader on multiple levels. It allows the writer the ability to move within time, space, and knowledge in a way that uniquely conveys the story.

For instance, the all-knowing narrator knows that Grendel can't be killed with conventional weapons, and we are aware of it, but no one in the story has a clue. That's because the omniscient narrator is privy to information the characters and reader don't have. Using an omniscient narrator is the only way to let the reader in on this information, while keeping the story flowing and tension building.

> **Super interesting side note:** the tension that comes from giving the reader information that the characters don't know is called *dramatic irony*.

One fantastic aspect of the omniscient point of view is its ability to present a story in a unique and interesting way, rather than having to start at the beginning and telling a story chronologically. Because of this, omniscient is often used to tell epic family sagas with dozens of characters because the narrator can impart information about each one. No single character is used as the window into the story, which can create multiple avenues of tension as the story unfolds. This also lends an opportunity to start a story in *media res* (a fancy way of saying mid-plot) because the writer can fill the reader in on all the details they need to know—past, present, or future—whether or not the characters ever learn them. This allows a writer to just drop the reader into the story without having to engage in a slow buildup. Not that a slow buildup is bad. It's just that it's nice to have a little variety in ways to tell a story.

In this way, using an omniscient narrator creates unique opportunities to reveal information. For example, they could create chilling suspense in a murder mystery when the audience knows who the murderer is, but we're waiting for the detective to figure it out. We might learn that the main character killed the wealthy homeowner with a piece of poisoned Gouda, placing us on the edge of our seats as we wait to see if she'll kill anyone else with cheese before the hunky detective can figure out the case.

Third person omniscient was a favorite POV of the 19TH century, and authors such as Jane Austen frequently used it to deliberately set a specific tone and insight for the reader. It allowed a view into everyone in a family, their love interests, other townspeople, and even minor characters who were privy to information the reader would need to know as the story progressed. It also allowed Austen to make sweeping proclamations such as, "It is a truth universally acknowledged, that a single man in possession of a good fortune, must be in want of a wife." This famous first line of *Pride and Prejudice* shows the narrator's omniscient voice and effectively sets the reader's expectations as they enter the story.

The omniscient point of view gives a writer a powerful tool in which to quickly immerse a reader in a richly detailed storyline. Let's try this point of view in our example scene:

The Hollowed Howls Tavern had been standing since the early days of the Druin Wars. From the beginning, drinks were pushed across the bar with no questions asked. Hags and Weres and everything in between were welcomed without censure at this bar.

Kyrie had no clue of the bar's history, but she knew it was a favored drinking place for a myriad of strange creatures, and the anonymity of the crowded melting pot gave her a modicum of safety when she slipped through the saloon doors.

The bartender glanced up when she entered. In the soft light, his dark eyes looked almost black, and disdain crawled across his face as she slid into a seat. They stared at each other across the bar. She'd been careful to cover her tracks, but the bartender recognized her. She didn't know the Shadow Hunters had been following her for weeks or that the man sending an ale across the bar to another patron had been shown her picture moments before she'd come through his door. She shoved a hand into her pocket, fumbling for the amulet, wondering how much the bartender knew.

Across town in the Barbery Hotel, the woman's contact waited. He'd last seen her in the woods of Mayfair, and he hadn't told her then the depth of his worry about her mission. So, he waited and swore he'd let her know as soon as he saw her. His wait would not be rewarded, however, because that meeting in the Mayfair woods would be the last time he had an opportunity to warn her.

The power of the omniscient narrator is that they know

everything, from the minutia of the day-to-day to the history of the world. They can tell you the date and out of which materials the building your character is standing in was built, the motives of every creature in it, and whether the fate of the world is about to be decided by the unconscious actions of a woman who never honestly believed she'd be anything other than the only daughter born to an ancient clan of Seers. It knows each of your characters' back stories, including those of their ancestors and their progeny, and it decides when and where to impart that knowledge to the reader. In this way, the omniscient narrator has almost unlimited control of the story, making third person omniscient a potent tool.

We talked about third person limited previously. To compare, in third person limited, you can provide a character's backstory, but it will be limited to what your viewpoint character knows or can learn from others. For the main character to know the bar was established in the early days of the Druin Wars, she must either be told that information, or we have to accept that she already knows it. Using omniscient, we merely need the narrator to tell us how old the bar is. Information is given when it is needed and, in the hands of a skilled writer, it can also create dramatic tension in a multitude of ways.

Have we told you how much we love the omniscient narrator? We do. But it vexes us, as well. Keep reading to find out why.

As much as we love it, we have to admit that third person omniscient is the trickiest POV to pull off successfully. It offers a writer such a vast toolkit to work with. This really gives a writer almost unlimited space to be creative. It's intoxicating, really, being free to do almost anything you want to do in the telling of your story.

Alas, with freedom comes responsibility. And that's the main drawback of using the omniscient point of view. So much freedom gives a writer an almost unlimited number of ways to screw things up.

We want to show you how to use your power for good. It will make this section a little longer than the other point of view sections, but we think it's necessary. We'll talk about such things as establishing a strong voice, setting the tone, dialing up the right amount of intimacy in a scene, effective ways to reveal information, what genres work best with an omniscient narrator, and what genres do better without an omniscient narrator.

Are you comfortable? Let's do this thing!

The first thing to understand about third person omniscient is that while your narrator has access to everyone's thoughts, feelings, actions, backstory, medical history, bank statements, and any other piece of information they need, they don't have your main character's voice, or the voice of any character in the book, for that matter. However, some omniscient narrators' voices are so strong and unique, they read as if they are almost another character in the book or readers might assume it's the writer's voice. This means that the writer needs to figure out what voice they want the narrator to use throughout the story.

You know what we mean by voice, right? It's the overall style in which a story is told. It's a mixture of the vocabulary used, the richness of the prose, the dialect employed, the flow and pacing of sentences, paragraphs, and scenes, the story's tense, the rhythms and sound, even the nuance of the story's attitude. In a word, it's the personality of the storyteller.

Earlier, we mentioned *The Book Thief* and how its omniscient narrator is Death, who isn't a character in the book. If you've read the book, you know why this was a brilliant choice. If you haven't read the book—and we recommend that you do—you can probably imagine how the narrative voice was employed: direct, familiar with sadness and grief, stoic in how it faces events, somewhat formal, solid in its understanding of the way the world works... You get the point. Death is a familiar entity. Most of us can guess its personality. The choice of Death as the narrator was perfect for the telling of a story based on the historical reality of a young German protagonist in Nazi Germany.

One way writers get voice wrong in an omniscient point of view is by not giving their narrator a distinctive voice. In other points of view, the characters impart the voice, especially if first person is being used. It's actually hard to not develop a voice when you've done the work of putting together a character sketch for your characters. In omniscient, the narrator's voice is often as distinct as any character's voice, and the narration should reflect that. Putting together a sort of character sketch for your omniscient narrator, complete with motivation and other personality traits, may allow you to deploy a narrator who aligns smoothly with the intent of the story.

Then there is tone. In general, there are two main tones in literature: dramatic and comedic. Within those two main tones are subtones. The subtones can be formal and informal, deep or lighthearted, warm or cold, highbrow or lowbrow. Basically, any way you can describe a person's personality or attitude can be used to describe the tone of a story.

The narrator is what affects the tone of a story the most. Obviously, the physical descriptions, the feelings related, and the events that take place will affect the story, too. But what the narrator notices and how they react to what takes place set the tone more than anything else. For instance, death and divorce are very serious events, but if the narrator reacts with humor to either one, their serious nature is bound to be affected and possibly subdued.

In this way, the narrator sets the tone of a story. As with voice, writers can miss the mark when using an omniscient narrator by not defining a tone for the narrator. This results in a story with a bland ambiance, which can bore the reader or even confuse them, especially if the storyline is out of sync with the feel of the work.

Speaking about the "feel" of the story, another responsibility of the narrator is to control the intimacy of the various scenes. By this, we mean point of view plays a very important role in how close or distant the reader feels from the characters and action. One cool thing an omniscient narrator can do is zoom in and out from any particular scene by employing emotion and sensory details to define the composure of the characters, the immediacy of the action, and the details of the setting. This is an enormous factor in the magic with which a good writer imbues their craft. Making a reader *feel* is the primary objective of most writers. It's the difference between a good story and great story.

When comparing intimacy within the points of view, first person and third person limited own the distinction of being the most intimate. This is because, in both points of view, the story is being told by an actual character who can tell the reader exactly what they are feeling, thinking, and doing. The reader is in their head. You can't get any more intimate than that. Omniscient is less intimate because there is a layer of remoteness inserted between the person telling the story and the characters. Rather than the reader experiencing even as if they are the character, they are still being told what's going on. In fact, it can be downright sterile if you're using third person objective, where any sense of opinion is removed altogether. A skilled writer using an omniscient point of view can dial up the intimacy by leaning heavily on "show, don't tell" advice, and use more sensory description and less exposition.

It's an artform. It really is.

The best advice we can give here is when in doubt, go deep. Get as intimate as you can and include thoughts and opinions of the characters. Readers rarely complain of being too close to the characters, but they will be the first to point it out in a review if they don't feel connected to them.

While just about every genre includes writers who have successfully written their stories in the omniscient point of view, some genres are better suited for it than others. Science fiction, fantasy, and horror are particularly suited to it. The main reason is the tension-building capabilities of an omniscient viewpoint. When the narrator can drop information at any point, they can time the reveals in such a way as to create heightened tension and incorporate suspension of disbelief in the best ways. In this way, dramatic irony can be used more readily than in many other points of view. A word of warning, though: a writer should avoid information dumps, which are easy to do in omniscient. Try to spread information out organically through dialogue and action rather than through information-dense narratives.

Conversely, writers in some genres should be cautious about using an omniscient point of view. The one that comes to mind before all others is romance. There are a few reasons why it is not the best point of view to use, the first being that while omniscient is all-knowing, it is still third person, and by definition, aside from third person limited, third person has a barrier between the character and the reader. Romance relies on a very deep intimacy to connect the reader to the story and the characters.

Truth Bomb: A lot of publishers aren't that excited about an omniscient point of view, especially by first-time writers. Primarily because it is so flexible, it is difficult to maintain a tight narrative, especially when it comes to making sure the reader knows whose thoughts and emotions are being experienced, also known as head hopping, which we speak about briefly in the next section. So, it's good to know that, even if you are able to use omniscient in an effective way, you may have a hard time getting past the first step of a pitch, before the publisher or agent reads a single word of your story, and they note that you're using omniscient point of view as stated in the query email. Don't let this put you off, though. Just knowing some of the pitfalls should help you manage this very powerful point of view.

We've covered quite a bit regarding the omniscient point of

view. It's pretty cool, huh? There's so much you can do with it, and there are a few things to be aware of, so you don't fall into difficulty if you decide to experiment with it.

Now that you know more, you can knock people's socks off—give the omniscient narrator a try. Don't fear it. The best way to learn how to use it is to read books in the omniscient point of view and try it yourself. You'll get better with practice and feedback.

A note about head hopping…

We discussed **head hopping** in the previous section, so we wanted to go into a little more detail here, after the omniscient point of view section, since omniscient is the most susceptible to it. Head hopping is when a writer moves from being inside one person's head and then moves to another character's head without using a scene break or some other hint to let the reader know they are changing the point of view, giving the impression of hopping from one mind to another. This can ruin a story because it forces the reader to figure out whose perspective the narrator is telling the scene from. It can be a very disorienting experiencing that pulls the reader out of the story.

The bartender glanced up as Kyrie walked into the bar. In the soft light, his dark eyes looked almost black, and disdain crawled across his face as she slid into a seat. Her breath caught in her throat. She focused on keeping her face impassive, not giving into the fear.

The bartender suspected she had the amulet. She'd

been careful to cover her tracks, but he was clever, and Shadow Hunters were everywhere. He'd been following her for weeks before she finally managed to shake him off in the last town. Now she was here.

She forced herself to meet his gaze as a war between a desire to run and a desire to find out the truth raged in her head.

Here, the point of view is moving from Kyrie to the bartender and back like a ping pong ball, and it's difficult to know who is watching and who is experiencing each action. Worse, as the reader you don't know who you are aligned with. Who is the protagonist, and who is the antagonist? What a mess.

Try it yourself

Retell the story of *Hansel and Gretel* through the point of view of an omniscient narrator. Many fairy tales are already told through the omniscient point of view, but it would be cool to hear what the woodcutter was feeling and doing while his kids were lost in the woods. What was the witch thinking? Is it possible she's been being misrepresented all this time? Was she merely protecting her delicious cottage from trespassers? Or was she possibly even worse than we were made to believe? Maybe she was in cahoots with the woodcutter's wife!

Frequently Asked Questions

What are the types of point of view?

- First person

- Second person

- Third person

  ○ Third person, limited

  ○ Third person limited, multiple character

  ○ Third person, objective

  ○ Third person, omniscient

How do you know which point of view is best for your story?

The short answer to this question is three-fold:

1. Point of view is whoever the author chooses to tell the story.

2. The point of view may require a specific person or persons who provide the right information at the right time in the story.

3. It should provide the intimacy and tone the writer wants to convey.

Hopefully, the same point of view addresses all of these points. If it doesn't, the writer needs to make a choice.

Can you use more than one point of view in the same story?

Very few rules in writing are absolute. Writers throughout the ages have taken a chance and changed points of view in the same story and been successful with it. There is no way of knowing how many others took the chance and failed, though.

If you're asking this question, our advice is that you probably shouldn't. It's best that you become adept at using individual points of view before deciding to mix more than one in your story. But, because we have made a point to tell you repeatedly that rules are made to be broken, if you do decide to use more than one point of view, you should make sure to stick to one per chapter, or per delineated section within a chapter, to make sure your reader doesn't get lost trying to figure out who is telling the story, i.e. to avoid head-hopping.

What happens if you write most of your story in one point of view, only to determine it won't work for the climactic scene?

You basically have two choices: 1. go back and rewrite the story to use the point of view you need to make the climactic scene work, or 2. change the climactic scene to work with the point of view you initially chose.

This situation is more common than most writers want to admit. In fact, one of the authors of this book (Hint: it wasn't Finnian) rewrote her first book several times before it was published for this very reason, and we used the word 'several' because she literally lost track of how many times she had to do it. We also had to remove a curse word from this paragraph because she definitely has feelings about this fact.

What is the most popular point of view?

Before the 1900s, almost all best-selling novels, fiction as well as nonfiction, were written in third person. There were obviously exceptions, but third person was the method of choice. This is one reason literature from the previous eras seems more formal and is often interpreted as the classical style.

Third person is still the most used point of view overall, but in recent years, first person and second person have shown up more often and become more popular in certain genres. For instance, you will often see young adult fiction and memoirs written in first person, and many self-help and how-to books are written in second person.

Should I use the omniscient narrator?

We say yes! Try it, even if for just a short piece of fiction. If you aren't sure how to start, try writing, "Once upon a time."

Fairy tales are often told in an omniscient point of view, and starting your story with the old standby can help get you into the mind frame of the omniscient point of view.

World-building can certainly be easier when using an omniscient narrator. While your main character may not know exactly how the water filtration system on your world works, your omniscient narrator knows everything. It's a fun exercise in craft and well worth exploring.

Isn't the omniscient narrator just an excuse to head hop?

While it presents a greater risk than other points of view toward head hopping, no one really wants to head hop. It confuses the reader. A major key to avoiding head-hopping involves being clear when the point of view shifts from character to character. Make sure there are context clues to let the reader know when the narrator has moved focus to a different character. Try to shift at a chapter, section, or at least a paragraph break. Anything less can feel like whiplash to the reader.

What are some more examples of this point of view?

Anything from Terry Pratchett's *Discworld* series.

Carrie by Stephen King

Their Eyes Were Watching God by Zora Neale Hurston

Station Eleven by Emily St. John Mandel

The Chronicles of Narnia by C.S. Lewis

Stardust by Neil Gaiman

All the Light We Cannot See by Anthony Doer

Recommended Resources

Point of View: How to use the different POV types, avoid head-hopping, and choose the best point of view for your book (Writers' Guide Series) by Sandra Gerth, Ylva Publishing, 2016.

We love the Reedsy Blog in general, and their information on the omniscient narrator is divine. Check it out for more information.

https://blog.reedsy.com/guide/point-of-view/third-person-limited-omniscient/

Discussion Time

Check out our video in which Kimberly and Finnian talk about point of view and other Super Important things
https://youtu.be/kkse7tDcfi8

Try It Yourself

We've provided Try It Yourself exercises for each of the points of view as we've gone along, so let's try something fun.

Using this writing prompt:

The first time at a concert without parents

Write a short story from each of the following points of view:

First person

Second person

Third person

Third person, limited

Third person, limited, multiple character

Omniscient

Setting

Setting—The basic geographic location, timeframe, and environment in which your characters live.

The house smelled musty and damp, and a little sweet, as if it were haunted by the ghosts of long-dead cookies. — **Neil Gaiman,** American Gods

Introduction

It's Super Important not to let setting become an afterthought when crafting your novel because setting has an indelible impact on the plot and on the reader on many different levels. You can have the best plot and the most captivating characters, but if you don't have a developed setting, some readers may not feel grounded in your book. And when a reader feels ungrounded, their attention will be on trying to figure out where they are rather than on the plot. Have you ever read a book in which you felt like you were dropped right into the story, immersed in such a way that you could almost smell and taste the scenery? When you finish the book, you feel a sense of leaving a comfortable place you've grown to know.

We remember the first time we walked through New Orleans with Anne Rice's vampires, the smell of flowers and humidity unsuccessful at masking the underlying stench of humanity they walked among. Or the time we relaxed on the beach near the lighthouse, the scent of the tide, salty and fishy, heavy in the air even as the gentle breeze moved over our skin.

Setting can almost be seen as another character in your story, always present, always escorting the writer, the characters, and the readers through the wending path of plot. The personality of place is as important to a reader as the physical details and, as such, helps the reader to feel the emotion of a scene as much as the actions and thoughts of a character do. If a writer can seamlessly weave the setting and characters into a believable, fully developed scene, a reader can immerse themselves in the time and place of a story and fully acquiesce to the suspension of disbelief, which is the ultimate goal of any writer.

As you plot your novel, setting should be a conscious element you'll use to tell the story. It's more than just the place in which your characters stand. It's the fabric that the characters exist within as they make the journey they've been asked to travel.

The location will inform your characters and their development. If your story, for example, is set in Phoenix, Arizona, don't plan on having grand, sweeping scenes in which your characters dance in the rain—that is, unless it's during monsoon season. If your story is set in a small mountain town in the wilds of British Columbia, your characters probably aren't going to go to a concert or a fancy restaurant without making plans that include an hour long drive through the mountains to get to a bigger town with those kinds of extravagant amenities. A hotel stay will probably be involved, and you'll need to address whether it's okay to have them share a room.

Your setting affects how the characters sleep, what they eat, where they work, and what they do for fun. It can affect small things such as where they shop or huge things such as whether they'll likely experience violence, racism, homophobia, or sexism on a regular basis. If your plot is based around your main character searching for a magic amulet—ahem—you'd better have established magic in your setting, or your reader is going to have trouble suspending their disbelief.

Setting gives life to your story, it places your characters where they belong, and it gives the reader a way to follow along when your characters move. And as your characters change, so may their setting. Perhaps part of your setting is your main character's beautifully appointed loft apartment in Manhattan. Your main character is going through an extreme bout of depression and hasn't been able to wash a dish or sweep the floor in weeks. As their depression gets deeper and darker, so too may the setting get darker along with the character's mood. Maybe the windows get dirtier, blocking sunlight. In this case, the setting might be used to parallel the character's journey both into and out of the pit of depression.

The setting can also be used to create contrast with the characters. Perhaps the main character is a motivated, successful person whose life is always in control, but they live in a hundred-year-old house that is constantly falling apart. Here, the setting can be juxtaposed with the character's personality and used to create conflict or humor. Or perhaps you have a sunny, cheerful character who lives in a haunted mansion.

Your setting can be an exotic and elaborately designed world complete with new languages, cultures, and histories; it can be a place you've been a hundred times before; or it can be barren, reflecting your character's bleak existence.

We're drawn to remember the sensory experience that was Richard Matheson's novel *What Dreams May Come,* where the scenery told more of the story than the characters did at times.

Almost any scene in the book is a good example as the novel successfully takes the reader through a number of settings, literally between heaven and hell. However, to give a specific example, let's take the scenes in hell. These scenes present a harsh and violent setting that allows the reader to almost experience the agony, both physical and mental, of the character Chris as he tries to save his wife from having to experience it. The setting itself—hell—adds almost immeasurable emotional and physical detail before a word of description is used. These scenes are the penultimate sequences that tell the reader what the book is about—love conquers all. The main character loves his wife so much he is willing to risk anything, including hell, to prevent her pain. It is an extremely evocative use of setting, using place and related action to inspire emotions that immerse the reader. The setting was so well crafted in the novel that it was a primary reason the book was adapted to a movie, which won several awards for visual effects and design. Your setting doesn't have to be perfectly matched to your characters, but it should be intentional. As we're fond of saying, "You can do anything as long as you can do it well."

What's It All About?

Readers need a sense of place. Think about it. You come home from a day out and say, "Hey, I saw Bob today at the grocery store!" You've grounded your audience in a small way by giving them a place. You might say, "I saw Bob today at the grocery store. I have no idea why he was wearing a tuxedo at 7 am, but there you go." Now we have two setting markers—time and place.

It's important to think about setting as having layers in the same way your plot and character development happens in layers. There are no hard and fast rules to how you should unfold your setting, though it is good to give your reader a clear sense of where the reader is in the first couple of paragraphs.

Truth Bomb: Setting is one of the best ways to show, not tell. A writer has a wonderful opportunity to show their characters interacting through setting, as we described earlier in our example of the scenes depicting hell in the book *What Dreams May Come*. This can help an author avoid more expository writing, when they might inadvertently fall into a telling, not showing, mode.

So, now you should know that setting goes beyond the town where your characters live. We like to think of setting as everything that exists around your characters. So, how can we break it down to make it a little easier to add to your writing?

Let's look at the layers of setting, what they mean, and how you can best add them to your work to create a richer environment.

Place on a macro level

A macro level could mean the city or neighborhood where your characters live. It could be the planet or universe they inhabit. Before you begin your novel, you should have a basic idea of where your main characters call home. Consider where the story takes place, where the main characters are originally from, and how that has affected their lives. While setting may not seem as important as plot or character development, a main character who was raised in a rural town on a self-sustaining commune is going to have different sensibilities than someone who was raised in the French Riviera in a mansion with a pool and staff.

Considering your story's premise, are there certain physical details that might be important to the plot? Are there landmarks or special holidays/celebrations that might be unique to the people there? Is there a subway system? Minimal technology? Advanced technology? Communication limitations? Is the area known for having the absolute best roadside stand selling tamales at 3 am?

Once you know where your book is set, you can start thinking about which important aspects of that setting might make their way into the book.

Are you in Paris? Are you going to talk about the Seine, the Eiffel Tower, high-fashion shopping, or the abundance of clean water drinking fountains that can be located through phone apps?

Are you in Cleveland, Ohio? Do your characters live in the suburbs or the city itself? Are they in the downtown area, in a loft? Do they go to the Westside Market? Do they hang out in cafes in Ohio City? Maybe they have a framed photo of the Terminal Tower in their living room or some postcards from the Field of Corn sculptures in Dublin, Ohio, because their family went to it once on a road trip when times were good.

Some people worry about portraying a real place incorrectly, and that worry is not unfounded. People familiar with the area may be unable to enjoy the book because they can't suspend disbelief after an error takes them out of the story. Readers have a unique talent for spotting inconsistencies or mistakes, and some might even talk about them in reviews. If this is a worry, research is key. Or you can get creative and build a fictional world. You can even go with something in the middle and pick an existing place such as British Columbia, Canada, and make up a town within that province, giving you some freedom to create a fictional setting without worry of unintentionally getting something wrong.

Are your characters from another planet or an alternate universe? You have far more freedom than people writing in established locales because your world exists only in your mind, and you can construct it any way you want to. This can also cause you a lot of work in order to make the setting richly enough embellished to make it believable. It's more than just a spot on the map, it also includes landmarks, customs, weather, time aspects, special events, and many, many other unique details that make up a place.

All of the above is what we mean by place on a macro level. These details build up a believable setting in which our characters can relate to other people or function in the story. For instance, if your main character is LGBTQ and living San Francisco, California, they are far more likely to have a comfortable life with friends and in finding acceptance than a character in a place where a person can still be arrested or put to death for being queer, and the plot of the story will show this. A story of a young, single gay man who meets the love of his life can be a very different story based on your choice of locations for setting.

So, depending on how realistic you're aiming for, a little research and familiarity with your location will go a long way, and the Internet is a great resource.

Once you've established the overall place, you can move on to more specific details.

Place on a micro level

You know your main character lives in New York City. Now, it's time to bring it down to the micro level. Do they have an apartment? Is it tiny? (Note: Part of your research must include housing prices. A character who works in a bookstore and lives in a small town in Michigan might own their own home. That same character in Toronto, San Francisco, or New York probably can't afford to live without roommates even in a small space.)

On the micro level, we get into your character's bedroom, how they decorate, whether they like a blue and yellow color combination for their bathroom. Here, we'll find out that your character frequents thrift stores and decorates in the bright oranges of 70s retro style or that they've inherited their grandmother's antiques.

Here, you'll impart details such as whether they own a car, take the bus to work, or ride their bike everywhere and, if so, where they keep it when they're not riding it. If your character lives close to their workplace, maybe they walk to work, in which case, they probably have a backpack or some kind of bag for carrying the things they need for the day.

If they live in a big, sprawling city such as Phoenix, they may have a long commute. That may determine what kind of car they drive, which is also part of setting.

Beyond the home and workplace, place on a micro level means setting the scene of your main character's favorite stores, their gym, their best friend's home. Where your character lives affects where they hang out. Do they have a favorite coffee shop? Is there even a coffee shop in their town? Do they go to a fast food restaurant for breakfast every morning? Do they enjoy nature?

The details of location will start to naturally develop as you're working on your character development. If your main character is a vegan who goes to protests calling for more action on climate change, she may not own a car, or if she's rich, she may own an electric car or a hybrid. An executive might have a car service. This will also inform where they spend time, what kind of events they go to, and how far they will go outside of their neighborhood.

Sensory details

Though you may establish your sense of place before you start writing, many of the details of your setting will likely come as you're writing the book. A major part of setting is comprised of the smells, sounds, and sights around your character. You'll establish these things in your major settings such as your character's domicile, their workplace, and maybe their favorite pastry shop. And don't forget to think about these details as your character travels, whether they're just commuting to work, going for a walk in a park, or taking a beach holiday.

The sensory details that come from sight, sound, smells, taste, and touch can help create a rich experience for the reader and give your characters a deeper, more authentic life. As you're working through your manuscript, think about the environment in each place your characters visit or pass through.

Maybe they walk past a hotdog stand each afternoon and delight in the savory smells of sautéed onions and garlic. Perhaps they have to drive past a dog food factory on their way to work, and they roll up their window every time. Maybe the scent of lavender reminds them of a special time or person.

Do they hear a cacophony of traffic when they open their window? Do they wake up to birds chirping?

Sometimes, an author's descriptive power comes through in a passage about the colors of a farmer's market; sometimes, it might be just one color—a flash of blue that catches your character's eye.

We're not saying you need to load your manuscript down with pages and pages of nothing but descriptive prose about the setting. (Though, yes, some authors do this, and some even do it well.) We're suggesting that you consider what they might be seeing, smelling, hearing, and touching in each scene, and you can use the information provided by these details to initiate emotion or reaction. Remember Forrest Gump's blue-checked shirt? He seemed to wear a version of it in each scene in which he showed major personal growth, a small but meaningful detail in a movie absolutely brimming with small but meaningful details.

Paying attention to sensory details allows your character to live. It lets them experience the wonder of crisp, clean sheets and super soft blankets. It gives them the luxury of sitting on a freshly mowed lawn, smelling the cut grass and flowers, while hearing the low sound of a neighbor's radio playing 70s music.

Example:

The bartender glanced up as Kyrie walked into the bar. In the soft light, his dark eyes looked almost black, and disdain crawled across his face as she slid into a seat. Her breath caught in her throat. She focused on keeping her face impassive, not giving into the fear. Did he know she had the amulet? She'd been careful to cover her tracks, but the Shadow Hunters were clever, and they were everywhere. One had been following her for weeks before she had finally managed to shake him off in the last town. She had to suspect the bartender could be one, too.

She forced herself to meet his gaze as a war between running and finding out the truth raged in her head.

Here, we have some setting—we know the main character is in a bar and the lights are dim. But what if we could give her just a little more to experience?

The bartender glanced up as Kyrie walked into the bar, shaking rain from her cloak and hair. The soft light cast by the fireplace in the corner made the man's dark eyes seem almost black. Disdain crawled across his face as Kyrie slid onto a barstool. She focused on keeping her face impassive, not giving in to the fear. From the corner of her eyes, she noticed a group of hooded figures drinking from heavy steins. The acrid smell of sweat and horses assailed her nose. They were riders, then, and they'd come a long way. She stared at the glaring bartender, waiting for him to take her order. Did he know she had the amulet? She'd been careful to cover her tracks, but the Shadow Hunters were clever, and they were everywhere. One had been following her for weeks before she had finally managed to shake him off in the last town. The bartender could be one. Kyrie stretched in her chair, leaning closer to the fire. She might be in trouble, but at least she was warm for the first time in weeks. She forced herself to hold the bartender's gaze as a war between running and finding out the truth raged in her head.

There's nothing wrong with the first passage. In fact, it tells us a lot about the main character, her quest, and the challenges she's facing in just a few short sentences. But adding some sensory details gives more of a sense of the scene—it allows the reader to experience it along with the character.

Time

Time is of the essence, or so we've heard. It's certainly important in your story. And time can mean so many things in your story. It can set the pace, give a sense of urgency, build tension, relieve tension, indicate the tone of a scene, and provide hints about a character's abilities. A brief mention of the date can set an entire scene. *They walked in the park and talked about the colorful foliage* changes considerably by simply adding the season. *Each fall, they walked in the park and talked about the colorful profusion of foliage.* The light, smells, sounds, colors, and textures are all impacted, and you don't even have to describe them. You can guess they're walking on fallen leaves.

When thinking about time as part of your setting, consider it in the following categories.

The date

Date is important to your setting. If your novel takes place in Scotland in 1908, it's a different story than one set today. The date in which your story is set will determine so many aspects, such as whether your characters have access to running water, electricity, or cars. A novel set in 1989 won't have cellphones. If a story is set in the 1980s, it will require that only doctors and other on-call folks have pagers, but in a story set in the 1990s, a lot of people might have them.

If you set your book in an existing city, and you are using actual locales, remember to research to make sure they existed in the time in which your book is set. The date affects everything from food to clothing, from gender conventions to hobbies. Do people go to plays in the period in which your book is set? Did movies exist yet?

The date is what makes your book historical (generally understood to be set in the past by more than a decade or two), contemporary (set in the present), or science fiction (set in the future). And while you may have more leeway to invent situations of all kinds when writing a book that takes place in the future, you also have to consider the evolution of societal norms and political trends. What is the environment going to look like in one hundred years? For example, can you write a future novel set on Earth that doesn't consider the ravages of climate change?

The clock

Don't forget the actual hours (or minutes) when you're thinking about time. Though you don't have to be hyper-focused on the clock, it's important to think about it as you're moving your character through their day.

If you have your main character meeting a love interest for coffee and doughnuts at breakfast, and in the next moment, they're walking into their house saying, "Thank goodness the workday is over," we might get confused.

Further, the time of day may lend power to a certain scene. Are you looking to have a spooky, ominous scene? Maybe it takes place in the gloaming, that eerie time of day when it isn't yet full dark, but the daylight is disappearing. (Isn't 'gloaming' a freaking cool word?)

You may not keep track of every minute of your character's workday, but you should have a general idea of the time of day as you're writing your scenes, so the passage of time is realistic.

The season

Understanding the seasons goes beyond just a general idea that it's winter. Your seasons are dictated by the place and, in some ways, the date. Depending on where your book takes place, January could be a cold, gray bucket of suck, or it could be the nicest time of the year.

If your story takes place in the Virgin Islands in the summer months, your characters will be well aware of hurricane season. In Arizona, characters will know what monsoon season is and what steps to take for protection when one hits.

If your story starts in December in Winnipeg, how long can you go without mentioning the cold? Are they having a mild winter? Is there snow? Does your main character have to pull their windshield wipers off the windshield every night to make sure they don't become iced over and break?

The season can inform your character's mode of dress, their activities, their mental health, and even their weight.

The passing of time

Perhaps the most important aspect of time is the way it passes. If your story spans years or even just a few weeks, you will need a way to keep track of the passing of time. In a more complex story, this may involve using a spreadsheet with the weeks/months/years in your novel and the events that occur within them.

If you write a story that takes place over a few months, you'll want to at least keep a list of the dates when the story starts and how the time passes.

For example, if you write a story in which the main characters met each Thursday for a long-standing friends' date at a bar, you'd want to keep track of the days. It wouldn't make sense to have a Thursday meeting then, three days later, have another Thursday meeting. Trust us—someone would notice!

Truth Bomb: As much as your setting matters, it also matters *why* you set the story there. If you choose a specific, unusual location and time, the story should warrant it. Recently, we read a book that was set in 1985 in an unusual location, making us expect something specific to that time and place would happen, but it never did. In fact, the story rarely made mention of the locale or the things that made the 80s interesting. By the end of the book, we were more focused on why the author even mentioned the time and place if they had no significance to the story. If you're going to choose a special place or a special time, be intentional about it. Make sure your characters truly live in that place and embrace the fact that they're living in 1985. Otherwise, you risk distracting your reader from the story you worked so hard to write.

Summary

Ultimately, the amount of focus you put into setting is up to you. By now, you probably know our favorite piece of advice about writing—you can do anything as long as you do it well. Setting doesn't come naturally to some writers, and that's okay. It's far easier to add elements of the setting in revision than it is to go back and make a character authentic. If you feel more comfortable focusing on the macro level setting and going back during revisions to add sensory details or to make sure your timeline is accurate, that's okay.

If you've written your first draft, and you've gone back in with an eye specifically for the setting but still aren't sure if you've nailed it, consider asking your first readers to go through your story with an eye on place. Ask if they felt a sense of the characters' homes, of what time of year it was. Sometimes, having someone else read your work can help unearth those places that might need a little more (or a little less) detail.

In the end, it's a matter of balance, just like everything else. As you did in character development, you will research and learn far more about your setting than you will ever put in your book, but the more you learn, the richer your setting will feel. And that's what will keep the reader coming back to your work.

Frequently asked questions

Is attention to setting always necessary?

We always like to avoid over-generalizations. So, no. Setting isn't *always* important. But every story will have a setting of some sort. You can't avoid it. Even if you just note that your character is buying a coffee, you've established a setting. In some flash fiction pieces, the author may not spend much time developing the details of the setting, but they'll still provide small clues to give the reader a sense of place and time. So while a hyper-focus on setting may not always be important, it is impossible to avoid giving your reader some sense of setting. Since it's going to happen anyway, you may as well make it intentional.

I've set my book in a city I've never been to. What can I do to ensure a realistic setting?

Rolling up sleeves We are so glad you asked this. We have a lot of ideas about creating a realistic setting.

First, are you sure you can't take a trip there? A teeny one? No? Okay. It was worth a try.

If you can't go there, go to the Internet. You can research local coffee shops, where the movie theatres are, and how many stoplights are in the town. Blogs are a great source of information about a place because they can give a variety of points of view about the location, whether they're coming from a single individual's point of view, which can immerse you in the local customs and opinions, or a tourist/ government point of view, which might give more sanitized or general information. To find relevant blogs, you can start by casting a wide net by doing searches on the Internet with specific keywords identifying the location you're interested in, you can ask your friends, or search on specific blog hosting sites such as WordPress.com or Wix.com.

We like Google Maps when it comes to virtually visiting the place in question. There, you can wander the map looking for donuts, grocery stores, and the local library. Street View is a fantastic way to wander down the road and check out houses and such. A map can only take you so far—using Street View can tell you the things the map itself may not be able to tell you, such as whether or not there is a lot of pedestrian traffic, whether there are bike lanes, if there's room to push a stroller, and whether all the houses are painted the same color. You can use Street View to check out the parking lots of various shops. Is this important? It is if your main character drives a 22-foot sprinter van, and the local coffee shop they pop into only has four small parking places.

Facebook forums can also be a great source of information. Many cities have Facebook groups, and you can get information straight from the residents.

And speaking of residents, NextDoor is a great site for discovering the minutia of what people find important when talking to their neighbors.

You can use real estate sites to check out home prices in the area, both for sale and rent. Real estate sites are also a great way to investigate neighborhoods. What do the lawns look like in that area? What kinds of cars do people drive if they live on that street? What kind of political signs are displayed in the area? How many folks have swing sets in their yards or basketball hoops in the driveway? These are all small details that can bring authenticity to your setting.

YouTube can be another great source for research. Believe it or not, you can find actual videos of people simply driving through a city. We found this one of a person driving through Vancouver, British Columbia. https://youtu.be/3-6-my54ONk And while you might not want to spend an hour watching a city go by through someone's windshield, it could offer a lot of insight into your chosen locale.

Recommended Resources

We love this blog post by K.M. Weiland on keeping track of time in your novel. https://www.helpingwritersbecomeauthors.com/keeping-track-of-time/

Discussion Time

Finnian and Kimberly talk about why setting is like another character in your novel.

Go here to watch the videos:

Setting Pt 1: https://youtu.be/lYEbCBJkz1k

Setting Pt 2: https://youtu.be/QcDBCjqSeHg

Try it Yourself

For all writers:

Take a section of a story you wrote and, using different colored highlighters, pick out location, time, and sensory details (sight, smell, sound, taste, and touch). Are there some you use more than others? Do you show more or tell more?

Character Sketches

Character Sketch—The system of outlining your characters' traits, tics, speech patterns, and other defining characteristics, so you can not only stay consistent in your writing but also create authentic characters your readers will grow to love.

When writing a novel, a writer should create living people; people not characters. A character is a caricature.—**Ernest Hemingway**

Introduction

Some people craft full-on thirty-page outlines for each major character, with lists of everything from the brand of toothpaste they use to the fact that they once wet their pants in first grade, and everyone laughed at them. And some people just start writing with only the basic idea of who their main character might be.

We're not here to say one way is better than the other. But we do recommend at least trying to outline some basic information about your major characters before you start your novel.

There are a few important things you need to know before you start diving into your characters' lives. These can be as basic as:

How old are they?

What do they look like?

What will they have to overcome to get what they want?

What do they do for a living or in their spare time?

Do they have a best friend?

Or they can be more in-depth:

Do they prefer dogs or cats?

What is their worst fear or major flaw?

Who would they save in a zombie apocalypse?

What were they thinking when they chose a revolver as their weapon in the zombie apocalypse, when there was a machete right next to it? Don't they know ammunition is finite, and you need to cut off the heads of the zombies? Did they forget all their training? Really? What were they thinking?

Sorry. We got a little carried away there.

Anyway, while you don't have to know every little detail of

your characters' lives down to the brand of toothpaste they use, or whether they have the damn presence of mind to select the machete in the upcoming zombie apocalypse, you should at least know basic information about them. After all, plotting and character development go hand in hand. When you started plotting your novel, you probably already asked yourself what your main character wants and why they aren't currently able to get it. That's a first step to creating an authentic character.

Creating a character sketch does two major things. First, it gives you, the writer, a guidebook of sorts, so you can stay consistent in the external details of your character to their more subtle characteristics. If you're in chapter thirteen and are about to have your main character's best friend leave for work, but you suddenly can't remember what kind of job the best friend had back in chapter three—or was it chapter five?—you can flip to your handy character sketch to find out. This works for all sorts of details you might need to refer to over the course of writing your novel.

The other major reason detailed character sketches are useful is for making sure your characters *stay* in character. The more you know about your characters, the less likely it is you'll have your characters do something they probably wouldn't do. You'll know how they react in various situations your plot places them in. For instance, when your bozo main character's revolver runs out of ammo, instead of doing something smart to protect themselves, it's more believable that they will stand there with their finger up their nose while the zombies capture them and eat their brains or their best friend swoops in to save them, instead.

The more time you spend on your character sketches in the

beginning, the more of a feel you'll have for how each character will react in certain situations.

What It's All About

So, how do you start putting together a character sketch?

A character sketch is simply a written list of attributes a writer assigns to a character in their story. They can be high level, containing only enough information to identify them in a line up, which is where the "sketch" in character sketch comes from, or they can be very detailed to the point of having back stories or deep psychological profiles that never get mentioned in the story.

The level of detail you chose to go to in your character sketches often depends on how you come up with your story ideas. If you've already started working on an outline of a plot, you probably already know at least a few of the characters who will be in your story and the type of person they need to be to advance the plot along. In this case, you may already have an idea about what those characters are like, but you might not have a formal character sketch started. Or maybe your stories are more character driven, and you intend to build the plot around the fascinating character you have crafted in your mind. Many book series are built around characters like this, such as J.K. Rowling's *Harry Potter* series, Veronica Roth's *Divergent* series, and all the characters in *Game of Thrones* by George R. R. Martin. Because the actual characters are as important to the story as the plot is, if not more important, you'll want to be very specific about the details of the character. Having an in-depth character sketch may be necessary to keep track of details to ensure the character remains consistent and authentic.

The key word to both kinds of character creation is "authentic."

There are different ways you can go about putting together an authentic character, but first it's good to know that it's not the level of detail that's required for authenticity, it's the intentionality of the detail that matters. Authenticity is measured on whether the traits you assign to the character are believable to the role the character plays in the story. This is the genesis of the phrase "staying in character." For example, if the role of the character is to save the world, the character must possess traits that a savior of worlds might possess. So, one might assume bravery and strength might be traits that are important for saving the world. But what attributes does the character need to possess to accomplish the specific tasks required to save the world? Is the danger coming from a madman ensconced in a remote hiding spot protected by an army of massive beasts or a series of physically challenging tests? Well, then bravery and strength are probably good aspects of the character. But what if the danger is from a computer program or an asteroid hurtling through space? In that case, saving the world might require an expansive knowledge of computer programming or physics. If that's the case, a physically weak and terrified character could essentially reprogram the computer or figure out the velocity and trajectory of a threatening mass headed toward the Earth and save the world.

Regardless of how you come up with characters, there are a few things to keep in mind when you create them. All characters should:

- Have a specific role in the story—they propel the story forward; if they don't, don't include them

- Have their own character arc—with motivations, goals, and conflict

- Have a unique voice—different to that of any other character in the story

- Have basic physical characteristics described

- Have a backstory—even if it is mostly only known to the writer

- Be revealed over time—avoid information dumps

Main Characters—Main characters play a significant part in the overall plot. If they didn't exist, there wouldn't be a story. A main character will appear in most scenes.

Secondary Characters—These characters specifically support or act as barriers to the main character as the plot progresses. They provide the main character with some sort of catalyst that moves the story forward, and they probably have dialogue.

Tertiary Characters, or the Extras—Typically, tertiary characters appear more as setting than they do as unique characters. They may be townspeople, someone who played a part in a main character's past, or a character who makes a brief appearance to provide information needed to progress the plot. If they don't progress the plot or give depth to the story, don't include them. Many won't have dialogue, and if they do, it's brief.

The plot and sometimes the genre will determine how many characters are needed in any specific story. For instance, a romance will require at least two characters. Sometimes other elements will factor into how many characters are needed to tell the story. For instance, some stories need multiple points of view to successfully convey the storyline; therefore, the writer will employ multiple characters to tell the story. One thing to keep in mind is not to add unnecessary characters. The way to avoid it is to make sure each character is required to advance the plot, either directly or indirectly. If they don't advance the plot and are simply interesting, don't add them. They will only detract from your story.

All stories have at least one main character or protagonist. Examples of stories with only one main character are *Into the Wild*, *Castaway*, and *The Metamorphosis*. Most stories have two main characters, often a protagonist and an antagonist but not always. Examples of stories with two main characters are *Tom Sawyer and Huckleberry Finn*, *The Hours*, and *Romeo and Juliet*. And some stories have multiple main characters. Examples of stories with multiple main characters are *Stand By Me*, *The Big Chill*, and *It*.

Sometimes it can be hard to come up with compelling characters, and sometimes writers have no problem creating interesting characters, but the main thing is to make sure the character is actively moving the story forward. Once you determine what the character's role is, it usually becomes easier to bring them to life with characteristics that make them perfect for the part they play.

How do you develop a compelling character?

Start with the basics. Why are they in the story? What

qualities do they possess that make them the perfect character for their role in the book? Once you've figured out these fundamental questions, there are many ways to develop them into fully formed and unique figures for your story.

Many people rely on their imagination to pull their characters together. Other people like to use other methods, and we'll list a few of them here.

Try the short story method—Some people like to develop their characters in a brief biographical format, as if they're writing an essay about a person. An example:

> *Kyrie Ir'Coven is a twenty-five-year-old tracker, who was born into the resistance on her home planet. Her family is part of a group of freedom fighters struggling to regain their kingdom from the Shadow Hunters. The family's crown jewel, a magic amulet created by Kyrie's ancestor, has been stolen, and Kyrie is sent with a team to bring it back. She's strong, capable, and sure of her skills as a tracker, but she is starting to lose faith in her family's struggle. When she meets and falls in love with a Shadow Hunter who saves her life, Kyrie must face the possibility that she is on the wrong side of the war.*

As you can see, this isn't a detailed character sketch, but it does give us an idea of who our main character is. As you start writing more of these, other details will emerge. Perhaps Kyrie has a best friend who seems bumbling and is always foiling her plans. Maybe the Shadow Hunter love interest never wanted to be part of the war and always dreamed of being a librarian. Perhaps the Shadow Hunter has a love of rare old magic books and always has a suggestion about where to look when Kyrie wants to research the history of magic.

Each of these character bios will play into the others, and the more you write, the more you'll go back to the others and add to them.

Base characters on people you know in real life—One of the easiest ways to create interesting characters is to make them like a person you know.

> **Pro tip:** Be careful to mix it up enough to give you plausible deniability if the character has an unflattering persona.

Base them on a celebrity—Is there a famous person whom your character resembles? Some writers make vision boards and cut out pictures of celebrities to look at as they're writing to keep them focused on staying true to the characters. This works particularly well if you're having trouble picturing your character. Just looking at a picture can help you focus in on them.

Interview method—Imagine you're sitting down with a character and asking them questions about their life. If you're interested in this method, why not make a big production of it? Give yourself a list of questions and sit in a comfortable chair with a cup of tea. You could even record yourself talking to yourself (as if the world needs more evidence that writers are, in fact, awfully strange).

Personality tests—Go to an online personality test site and answer questions in a way your character would answer them. Not only will you gain information while answering the questions, but the application will give you a report that gives insight about the character's personality.

Astrological reading—Give your character a birthdate and look up the astrological analysis.

And just for fun—**Tarot card reading**—If you know how to read tarot cards, do a reading for your character, or you can go to a psychic and ask them to describe your character.

Online character generators—There are a number of free online applications that will put together a set of character details. Some are completely random, and others allow you to enter a few characteristics to get started.

Character development worksheets—We've created a character development worksheet for you that you can find and download at https://inkstacks.com/inkslinger/character-sketch/. A copy is also found in Appendix 3 at the end of this book.

Example from *The Shadow Hunters*:

Character Name: Kyrie Ir'Coven

Physical Description:

25 years old

5' 7"—tall for women in her world

Short, light brown hair

Brown eyes

Faint scar on her chin

Solidly built

Clothing is coarse woven with leather straps, boots, and a wool cloak that is used for protection from the rain and as a blanket on her journey

Character Traits:

Intelligent—would rather read and study than pursue leisure or entertainment

Hardworking

Sensitive

Empathic

Strong

Confident

Quiet

Can be single-focused

Motivation:

To regain Castle Gorn and free the land of the Dimness. All her life, she has had the same dream each night in which she goes on a great journey to reclaim her family's rightful place in Castle Gorn, which was taken by Maxis in the Twelve-day Assault, and to restore her mother's rule over Gornheld.

Fears:

That she will not succeed, that more will die in the process, that she will never see her parents again.

Where they live:

In a tent village in the Forest of Alnight, at the foot of the mountains on the edge of Gornheld. The village moves occasionally when the Shadow Hunters remind its inhabitants that they are more or less banished.

Friends, Family, Pets:

Mother—Adeera, former Empress of Gorn

Father—Frederick

Uncle—Skarsgard

Elder/Teacher—Manswain

Best Friend—Soteria

Eldora—Kyrie's harpy eagle

If you're an artist, you could even draw your characters, but you don't have to have artistic talent to find images online that look like your character.

Bringing your characters to life:

Creating well-rounded characters is important to ensuring they are believable. Human beings are complex. We have personality quirks and flaws. We like odd things. We sometimes see ourselves differently than others do. We may be self-aware and understanding of what we do wrong, or we might be completely clueless. We may hate our bodies. We may absolutely love cats to the point of squealing each time we see one.

Your characters will be different from each other in a lot of ways. They'll look different, they'll have distinctive personality traits, and they'll have unique voices. An elementary school teacher may speak in short, clear sentences because he's used to speaking to little kids. A Southern grandma may speak slowly and call everyone "Honey." A teenager may use excessive slang and sarcasm. Some characters may use interjections such as "Well" or "OMG." A character might swear a lot. Or, also effective, you may have a character who doesn't swear at all and drops an F-bomb in the middle of a stressful situation, shocking the other characters.

Truth Bomb: You will (and should) know way more about your main characters than your reader will ever know. Look, we know that everything in your character sketches is Super Important information and you want to share it all with your reader. But just as you wouldn't overwhelm your reader with a bunch of backstory, you also don't want to dump a bunch of character traits on them. A great thing about doing in-depth character studies and compiling a bunch of knowledge about your characters is that you can release the tidbits of information as they become relevant.

In other words, your knowledge of your character is for you more than anyone else, and it will inform you about how your character will behave as the story progresses.

Summary

Character sketches are designed to bring your characters to life. Authentic characters are the key to a great book. And while readers will generally forgive issues with minor plot points, the major complaint we hear when people give bad reviews on a book is that the characters weren't realistic.

Good characters live and breathe, and to do that, they must have human traits. That doesn't mean they can't be supermodel slender or be muscled like the Rock. It does mean that beyond those muscles, they must have human flaws, real fears, and actual character quirks. It means their behavior in each situation must match the personality you've already set up for them.

Frequently Asked Questions

Do I have to have a character sketch for every character?

You only need a sketch for your major characters. Beyond that, use your own judgement. If that barista only shows up in a couple of chapters and doesn't even have a name, they probably don't need a character sketch.

On the other hand, if that barista drops a nugget of important information—perhaps they're a dog trainer, and your main character will ask them for advice about getting along with their new love interest's dog later in the book— you should keep track of that information somewhere.

For our part, we generally keep at least an informational sheet on any character who has a speaking part. Even if you just keep a file called "The Barista" and note they have blue hair and work as a dog trainer, you have the information should you happen to need it again.

What if I can't think of an answer to a question about a character?

Don't sweat it. The character sheet is a guide, not a test. You aren't going to fail if you don't know your main character's worst fear or if you don't want to think about their favorite alcoholic beverage. After all, you probably don't know every little thing about anyone in the world. Either the answers will come to you as you need them while you're writing, or you won't ever need them and won't have to worry about it.

What if I'm writing about someone outside of my lived experience?

Diversity is awesome!

The main thing to remember is to do your research. If you don't have depression, for example, and you're writing about someone with depression, research depression. Interview people who have depression. Make sure you're writing from a place of honoring that person's experience rather than exploiting it.

We love a wealth of lived experiences in a novel, and we fully believe there is space in a book for people from all sorts of religions, races, cultures, gender expression, orientations, abilities, etc.

Beyond research, there are a couple things to remember. One is that you can't expect one person from any group to stand in for every single member of that group. Reading about the experiences of a wealth of people from any group is important. Talking to a group of people is also important. And seriously consider hiring one or two sensitivity readers. If you're writing about a trans person, seek out trans people who are willing to read your book. And be open to changes. If your sensitivity reader tells you something is a stereotype and needs to be changed, look at what you've written and ask yourself why you wrote the character in that manner.

What if my character isn't likable?

For readers to keep reading, they need to be invested in the characters and want to see what happens next. They'll often stop reading if they don't care. It's possible to have an unlikable character if the point of the story is to watch the character get what's coming to them. However, if the character starts off as unlikable in order to go through a transformation by the end of the story, at some point you'll want to give the reader clues that the character is redeemable. Consider giving the character internal thoughts that indicate they have positive traits, give the reader glimpses of the character's goodness, or give the character dialogue , either internal or external, that indicates that they want to change. Giving the character fears or insecurities makes them human and more relatable, and your reader will hang on to see them become good.

Occasionally, when a reader says they don't like a main character, it's because they aren't connecting to them. You can fix this by fleshing out the character a little more by giving them relatable human traits and helping the reader develop empathy for them.

Resources

Write Characters your Readers Won't Forget by Stant Litore, published by Westmarch Publishing, April 2, 2015

The Art of Character by David Corbett, published by Penguin Books, January 29, 2013

Discussion Time

Join Finnian and Kimberly as they discuss character sketches

Character Sketches Pt 1: https://youtu.be/rykMix699fs

Character Sketches Pt 2: https://youtu.be/BYfpI_ClUxg

Do It Yourself

Pick one or more of the following:

1. Create character sketches of the main characters in your current work in progress.

2. If you don't have a work in progress, create a character sketch describing yourself or someone you know using the techniques we explore in this chapter.

3. Create a character sketch for the main character of your favorite book.

Tying It All Together

We're almost to the end of this journey. You've stuck with us this far, Dear Writer, and we're grateful for your time and attention. Remember, this book is a guide, and it gives you the tools you need to write your amazing book. The rest is up to you.

As we noted in the beginning, you may not go through all these chapters completely in order. You may find it more comfortable to come up with some great characters and plug them into a solid plot. Or you may start writing a plot and realize you're developing some awesome characters.

We're here to give you guidance, and to help you craft the best book that you can, but you're the boss of you. You get to decide the best way to make it work. As we said earlier, this isn't the only path to writing a book. But it's *a* path that gives you a starting point, and it works. Once you've gone through it once, you'll know what tweaks you need to make to your individual process, so it works best for you next time. You may find the entirety of this book works perfectly for you and follow it for everything you write. Or you might vibe with specific elements and leave the rest. We're okay with that. We just hope we helped you, though. We know how much writing means to us, and if we can make your writing any easier, we are happy.

If we can offer you the best advice to take away, it is this: There are numerous articles, social media posts, and videos claiming to share the path to becoming a real writer, but only you know what will work for you.

Know this: you *are* a real writer. If you're writing, if you're buying books like this to hone your craft, if you're doing things like creating character sketches and learning about plot structure, you're a real writer, whether you've published anything or not.

No one has the market on the best process for every person. If you're like us, you may find that some things work right now that didn't work for you last year, or even last month. Most writing advice will tell you to write every day to establish a routine. We're here for that. Finding a way to work on your writing each day does a couple of things. First, it helps you establish a routine. Even if you can only give fifteen minutes a day to your writing, you're still getting words down. It shows that you're serious. It's a tangible reason to be proud of yourself.

That said, sometimes life gets in the way, and you absolutely can't write every day. We know some writers—ahem, Finnian—who may not write at all for two weeks then sit down for an eight-hour marathon on a random Thursday, busting out thousands of words and coming out looking like that guy in the sleep-aid commercials before he got the good rest.

There's nothing wrong with that. As we said, you're going to find the process that works best for you, for now, and you'll gain the confidence to make changes as you need to.

Whatever your process ends up being, know that we're here for you. At Inkslinger, we'll continue to put out how-to books, helpful articles, and of course, our software platform designed to help writers get that novel written.

Now that you've got the tools, get out there and write that book. And please be sure to let us know when you have. We're over here supporting you and cheering you on!

Appendix 1—The Planning of *The Shadow Hunters*

As you may have noticed, many examples we have given throughout *Inkslinger 2—Planning Your Amazing Book* are for a book called *The Shadow Hunters*. The inspiration for *The Shadow Hunters* came to us while writing this book. So, as we provided examples within our text, the plan for our own awesome book began to take shape, which just goes to show you how inspiration can come at any time, from anywhere. In a way, we're demonstrating how helpful this book can be in planning your amazing book.

In this section, we will describe our experience of following our own advice.

Target audience

When we started planning *The Shadow Hunters,* we thought it would be a romance because that is the fiction genre we each usually write in. But when we started to plot and outline, we gravitated toward a genre that was more fantasy-than romance-based, and we realized we would have to re-evaluate our target audience to make sure we knew how to appeal to them.

Much of the knowledge we have from writing romances still applies to a target audience that reads fantasy, but there are some key differences. We won't bore you with too many details, but we'll discuss a few.

The first and probably most drastic difference is that our romance audience is predominantly female, while fantasy appeals to all genders. This means we need to be more aware of how we present our characters. We decided to have a female lead because fantasy books tend to have male leads, and we'd like to see a more balanced mix and give female readers characters they can relate to. In that vein, we also included a non-binary character because we care about diversity and representation. Because the world in our book is not on Earth, we didn't include skin color or ethnic diversity originally, but we decided that for the same reasons we find it important to include gender diversity, we need to include diversity in those areas, too. We spoke about using sensitivity readers in the character sketch chapter to make sure we portray diversity in a respectful and accurate way, and we intend to do that when the book is written.

Genre

We chose fantasy for our story. As you'll recall from the chapter on genre, our primary discussion didn't revolve around how to pick the genre but more about how the chosen genre might affect decisions about how you approach your book. The following describes what we needed to take into account because we chose a genre different to our familiar genre of romance.

There are different beats to a fantasy story

In the chapter on Plot and Outline, we discussed how most fiction books follow a set of seven plot points, **also known as beats: set up, the inciting incident, reveal the goals/ desires, introduce the opponent, rising action, climax,** and **resolution.** These are described in the 3-Act Structure. Fantasy books also follow that general structure, but some genres include additional plot points specific to the genre. Fantasy has its own subset, as does romance, our familiar genre. So, we had to learn the difference between fantasy and romance beats. This is what we found for the additional fantasy beats:

A central conflict that affects the entire world

Instead of showing unfulfilled desire in the setup, we had to show our character's desire to fix something that affects their entire world.

Magic and /or supernatural elements are what usually define a story as Fantasy

Instead of getting the two romantic leads to meet and fall in love, which defines a romance story, we had to establish how magic would play a part in our story.

Fantasy generally revolves around a hero

Instead of putting the two romantic leads at cross purposes in order to build the romantic tension, we had to work on establishing the characters as the potential heroes upon which everything in the story relies.

The setting of a fantasy novel often consists of fantastical elements

Instead of establishing a romantic encounter in which the two leads discover their feelings for one another, we had to create a setting that crackles with fantastical elements that lend themselves to helping the heroes succeed.

Power structures play a large role in fantasy books

And finally, instead of proving to the characters that they are meant to be together and therefore deserve a happily ever after, we needed to establish a power structure to be corrected.

Target audience

As we noted earlier, the target audience for fantasy books has commonalities as well as differences as compared to the target audience for romance books. Not only is it necessary for us to identify the specific demographics of those who buy fantasy when we begin our book marketing and promotion, but we have to figure out what appeals to the typical fantasy reader in the story itself. Beyond the expected beats we discussed above, fantasy readers tend to want storylines that are more action-oriented, with good versus evil and an intellectual element. Language is important. The tone is often moodier and can address intense social issues.

World-building

Fantasy stories rely on extensive world-building, and taking our own advice, we want to go well beyond the physical setting of the story. It might include creating new cultures, languages, species, technologies, even universes. If you know anything about *The Lord of the Rings Trilogy*, you know that J.R.R. Tolkien built a world so unique and believable that fans have devoted untold time and energy learning Elvish, one of the languages he created for the story, and have crafted replicas of Middle Earth to be used in elaborate cosplay. Fantasy readers and writers are serious about world-building. We can only hope we do it justice.

As you can see, just by moving to a new genre, we have to factor several aspects into our thought process and decision-making.

Point of view

While *The Shadow Hunters* could effectively be written in first person, third person omniscient, or third person limited, at this point, we plan to write it in third person limited from Kyrie's point of view. We chose this approach because Kyrie is the primary character, and knowing what she sees and thinks will be the best way to impart information as the story progresses. In addition, we may start writing and decide we want chapters from another character's point of view. That's far easier to do if we're already in third person limited.

Setting

As we've noted above, world-building is a major process in creating a believable setting/world for fantasy books, so we will be paying considerable attention to it. In *The Shadow Hunters*, the empire is a terrible place to exist for anyone except those in power. At the beginning of the story, you find out that the Dimness has fallen over the entire empire, as the life force is being leached from everything to give Maxis his power. Unrest is pervasive throughout the empire, people are starving, and the castle armies are attacking settlements with impunity. The setting needs to reflect this. We will focus attention on making this believable. For now, we have a brief description of the setting from a macro view.

The entire story takes place in the Kingdom of Gornheld, an island nation located in the Northern Seas. At one time in the not so distant past, Gornheld was a thriving empire made up of twelve settlements spanning the entire island, which would take a healthy adult thirty days to walk across from east to west and forty-five days from north to south. However, now, as the land has fallen into the Dimness, it could take a person more than twice as long to cross, for caution is more important than speed. Unrest is not the only danger, though, as the land has turned upon itself, and its surface has become a festering wound in many places, unfit for most life. The entities who can survive the worst of it are mean and will kill a person without a thought just so they don't have to compete for the meager sustenance still provided by the land.

Character sketches

The story was inspired by our example of Kyrie going into the tavern while she is on her quest to get the amulet back. From that example, we began to keep a character list and add to it after we wrote the examples for each chapter. It wasn't until we had to provide a character sketch in the Character Sketch chapter that we created a full sketch for Kyrie. Below is the list of characters we have so far, followed by Kyrie's detailed sketch.

List of characters

- Kyrie Ir'Covenmain character

  ○ Eldora—Kyrie's bird

- Adeera Ir'Coven—Kyrie's mother

- Frederick Ir'Coven—Kyrie's father

- Soteria—Kyrie's best friend

- Kassandra the Eye—seer/madwoman, can take the form of a cat

- Eldric—Shadow Hunter, all Shadow Hunters are non-binary

- Maxis—evil dictator

- Skarsgard Ir'Coven—Kyrie's uncle

- Manswain—elder assistant to Shamlin Joseph

- Shamlin Joseph—elder

- Orkney—another Shadow Hunter

Character Name: Kyrie Ir'Coven

Physical Description:

25 years old

5' 7"—tall for women in her world

Short, light brown hair

Brown eyes

Faint scar on her chin

Solidly built

Clothing is coarse woven with leather straps, boots, and a wool cloak used for protection from the rain and as a blanket on her journey

Character Traits:

Intelligent

Hardworking

Sensitive

Empathic

Strong

Confident

Quiet

Can be single-focused

Motivation:

To regain Castle Gorn and free the land from the Dimness.
All her life, she has had the same dream each night in which
she goes on a great journey to reclaim her family's rightful
place in Castle Gorn, which was taken by Maxis in the
Twelve-day Assault, and to restore her mother's rule over
Gornheld.

Fears:

That she will not succeed, that more will die in the process,
and that she will never see her parents again.

Where they live:

In a tent village in the Forest of Alnight, at the foot of the mountains on the edge of Gornheld. The village moves occasionally when the Shadow Hunters remind the inhabitants that they are more or less banished.

Friends, Family, Pets:

Mother—Adeera, former Empress of Gorn

Father—Frederick

Uncle—Skarsgard

Elder/teacher—Manswain

Best friend—Soteria

Eldora—Kyrie's harpy eagle

Plot and outline

The following is our current plot and outline following the 3-Act Structure. You'll see that we have a solid arc with some detail provided, but it isn't a complete story yet. The main points, such as the setup, some of the buildup, the crisis, and the end are there, but most of the finer points are still to be written. Fantasy books run anywhere from 50,000 to 150,000 words, with most closer to around 100,000 words, so there is a lot to write. And as we write the story, some of it will almost certainly change as we fill out the details and come up with additional plot points.

Plotting *The Shadow Hunters* in the 3-Act Structure:

Act I: The Beginning

Opening scene or prologue: *(We decided on an opening scene here because we are writing a frame narrative, and we have to set the scene for that.)*

An elderly person (the reader doesn't know this, but it is the Shadow Hunter, Eldric, who comes into the book later) sits at a campfire, talking to a group of children. They tell the children that it's important to hear this story because their world was once at war, and it was all saved because of one woman.

It starts like this: Once upon a time, a young woman named Kyrie Ir'Coven was chosen to sacrifice herself to save the world...

The setup: *Introduce your main character and give the reader a hint of trouble in their real world. Start world-building to create a believable setting.*

Kyrie and her parents live in tents in the Forest of Alnight in the foothills of the mountains at the end of the empire. The empire is at war, the empress has been deposed, magic has been outlawed, and factions are fighting. An overlord, an evil dictator, sits in the castle at Gorn. People are starving in the empire and being killed for minor offenses. Kyrie and her parents are part of a rebel faction seeking to restore the empress to the throne and bring peace back to the empire. They move their tent village from place to place when the Shadow Hunters escalate their attacks, and the Shadow Hunters have started another escalation. The village is restless. Kyrie patrols with the sentries, watching for attacks.

The inciting incident: *What takes your character from their current world into the new world?*

Kyrie turns twenty-five, her year of individuation, and her mother takes her aside and tells her that her family are the true rulers of the empire. Her mother also tells her the family's magic amulet was stolen by a traitor to the empire during the Twelve-day Assault, driving the empire to war, forcing Kyrie's family into hiding, and binding the magic of anyone who will not swear allegiance to Maxis. Kyrie's parents tell her the Dimness is on the verge of draining the empire of its life force, and it is up to her to travel across the land, disguise herself as a member of one of the rival factions, and steal the amulet back.

About the amulet: It has the power to enhance the magical power of whoever wears it. Because the evil overlord wears it, his power is amplified, draining the empire of its magic in order to supply power to the wearer. (Good people who wear it amplify goodness and love.) With the amulet in the hands of Maxis, the land is thrust into the Dimness. In addition, Maxis has bound the magic of anyone who has not sworn allegiance to him.

The village seer, who many consider a harmless fool, devises a plan to retrieve the amulet before the empire has been drained of its energy. (The seer retained her magic by acting as if she were a harmless peasant, and she cast a spell over herself right before all magic was outlawed and bound by the Assembly at an order issued by Maxis. The empress and others pretend the seer is crazy, so she isn't found and executed, but she has been their secret weapon in tracking what Maxis is doing and finding the right time to retake the throne.) She has had visions, and Kyrie's mother seeks advice from the top elder of the village, who agrees that it is time that the throne shall be retaken.

Kyrie, the only heir to the throne, is the person who has to make the journey to retrieve the amulet whose wearer, her mother, shall ascend the throne. Someone betrayed her family to the overlord who took over their kingdom. Kyrie is not surprised by the quest. She has had dreams all her life that she would make this journey, she just didn't know why. Now she does.

Kyrie and Soteria get ready for the quest, and Manswain, their elder and teacher, works to get them ready.

The Meet Cute (for romances): *The moment the two main characters first meet. In a non-romance, this can still happen. Perhaps the main character meets the antagonist or a mentor figure. (We can still have a meet cute, though this isn't a romance, because we're bringing in someone who will be a sidekick in this story, even though they won't be a love interest.)*

The meet cute in this story is the realization of Kyrie and Soteria's relationship being more than a friendship. This realization comes when they seek a reading from the seer, who tells them the true nature of their love and that they have two choices: refuse the quest and live together for the remainder of their lives (hinted to be short); or, go on the quest, save the empire, but one of them will not come back alive. Kyrie is certain the seer is referring to her because, in her dreams, she dies during the quest.

A little back story: Kyrie and Soteria are sort of platonic lovers. They have known each other from childhood. Neither is interested in being bound to a spouse, but they love each other in their way. Their relationship is not a traditional relationship, but their bond is accepted by the rest of the village. They are loyal to one another, inseparable, and would do anything for one another.

A sentry shows up here. Kyrie likes them but doesn't pay them much mind. (We find out this is Eldric, a Shadow Hunter who has infiltrated the village as a spy.)

The debate/second thoughts: The character debates whether they can succeed at obtaining their goal or desire and thinks about the consequences. They have doubts. They may start seeing things they really love about their current life.

Kyrie doesn't want to leave her village, nor does she believe in fighting. She's a pacifist. On the other hand, she loves her parents and wants to help them.

Act II: The Middle

The choice: *The main character makes a decision, and the reader starts to learn what price the main character might have to pay to take this journey.*

Kyrie and Soteria decide to take a chance and go on the journey. Manswain gives them paper maps of the land for their quest.

Side characters: *Develop side characters. Introduce or further develop subplots.*

Kyrie's parents work in the background to find out who the traitor is. They think Kyrie's uncle has been killed during the Twelve-day Assault, but really, he is the betrayer and is living the high life in the castle with the new dictator.

Obstacles: *What happens to keep the main character from reaching their goal? (It's good to have a brief triumph over this obstacle. It won't last.)*

Kyrie and Soteria run into the Shadow Hunters and are able to evade them. Kassandra the Eye, the seer and prophet, helps them in the form of a cat. The sentry they knew in the village assists them in evasion and joins them on the journey.

Relief: *A point in the story when everything seems to be going well. The main character starts to feel confident. They've won a small victory, and life is better.*

Having evaded the Shadow Hunters, Kyrie and Soteria proceed to Castle Gorn. Their travel through the Sway, the largest section of decay in the empire, is arduous. They meet many obstacles both natural and supernatural. The cat shows up on occasion to help them. A few times, it seems that magic helps them, surrounding them in violet light held within a mist. (It turns out later that this is Kyrie's magic beginning to come through.)

More obstacles: *After the first obstacle, the main character starts to feel they have a plan. This obstacle wrecks that plan and raises the stakes.*

Eldric has been shadowing them and plans to capture them right before they get to the castle. Kyrie knows this because she sees Eldric in her dreams. Kyrie is powerless to go against the natural flow of life, so, even though she knows what will happen, she can't do anything to change it unless it is willing to be changed. In this world, Fate is an entity.

Absolute disaster or crisis point: *This is the biggest obstacle, the moment when the main character loses everything they've worked for to this moment. It's the obstacle that makes your main character think the battle will never be won and all is over. Don't forget to give your main character some time to hate their life right now. Everything is lost (they think), and they'll never win. They deserve to have some time to wallow.*

Eldric thinks they are so smart, pretending to be a sentry,

and basically walking Kyrie and Soteria right into their imprisonment—or worse. But somewhere along the way, Eldric's feelings have changed, their alliance is in question. It shouldn't be. The Assembly's magic should have locked Eldric's loyalty to the throne, as they have with all the Shadow Hunters' loyalties. They have never had a choice. They serve the throne. Always have, always will. They question capturing Kyrie and Soteria, but the quest has been completed. No longer in Eldric's hands, it has to be carried out. Their task is to lead Kyrie and Soteria to their reckoning. As soon as they enter the grounds of Castle Gorn, the group is stalked by Skarsgard, and Eldric, caught in their own conflict, has to make a choice between revealing who they are and whether they should help Soteria and Kyrie when they enter the trap or making sure they stay captured. Ultimately, they don't get to choose. Skarsgard attacks while Eldric wages war with their loyalty. Everyone thought Skarsgard was dead, but Kyrie and Soteria find him in the castle controlling the evil overlord, Maxis, who is really the puppet of Skarsgard. Soteria perishes in the fight. Devastated, Kyrie escapes. Eldric tracks her and finds her grieving and questioning her choices. They try to get her to go back and finish Skarsgard and Maxis. But she can't find the strength and heads back to the Forest of Alnight, unafraid of death and without the amulet, giving up on her quest. Eldric goes with her, their loyalty to Kyrie growing more solid with every step away from the castle. The farther from the amulet, the less power it has over them. Before they get far, the cat appears, shows her the future, tells her Soteria's death would be in vain if she stops now, and she decides she has to try again with Eldric by her side. They have to figure out a way to keep the power of the amulet from controlling Eldric when they get closer to the castle. When they get to a point where Eldric feels the power taking over, they have to stop and let Kyrie go forward alone.

Act III: The End

Climax: *The moment of truth. It's the gut punch of the plot, when the main character either gets everything they want or realizes they're never going to get it. It's the moment the reader has been waiting for.*

Kyrie fights Skarsgard and Maxis. She's about to lose, but the cat shows up and claws Skarsgard's eyes out. He stumbles to the back of the room and falls out the castle tower window, dying on the ground below, but not before Kyrie finds that he has more than half of the amulet, which explains how he was able to control Maxis. Maxis gets hold of Kyrie and puts his hands around her neck to strangle her. But being so close to the amulet, Kyrie discovers her magic is very powerful. Kyrie rips the amulet from his neck, and it remolds itself back together. The Shadow Hunters descend upon them, and she throws it to the cat and says, "Get this to my mother, the rightful empress." (Animals can't rule, so even though the cat is Kassandra the Eye, while she is in cat form, the amulet does not give her the power.) With the amulet out of the castle, the Shadow Hunters are no longer bound to Maxis, and they tear him apart.

Eldric, no longer conflicted in their allegiance, rushes in and chops off Maxis's head, as Maxis is no longer protected by the amulet.

The Shadow Hunters drop their weapons, as they are now aligned with Kyrie. She doesn't wear the amulet, but she has the power of the throne because she has freed the empire from the darkness. The Dimness begins to fade.

Falling action: This allows you to wrap up any B stories and subplots. Maybe a little obstacle comes in here, but it's resolved easily. Falling action can help bring the reader down from the intensity of the rising action and climax.

Kyrie and Eldric make their way back to the Forest of Alnight, and the Dimness continues to recede. Their journey back is much different than the journey there. Peace is falling over the empire. Hope is returning. The very land is healing.

Processing: The characters get to talk about what happened. This allows the writer the opportunity to tie up loose ends.

Kyrie's mother puts on the amulet, and she is reinstated in Castle Gorn as the rightful empress. The empire continues to heal.

A major celebration, with a memorial for Soteria, takes place. Her spirit, with the help of Kassandra, joins the festivities and she tells Kyrie she will always be with her to protect her.

Denouement: The end. The characters live happily ever after, or they don't. Everything is completely wrapped up, unless there's a sequel, in which case, you might leave a dangling tidbit.

The elder who started the story finishes the story, and we see who it really is. They also explain why power did not move to the cat when it had the amulet.

The elder also explains that Kyrie is the rightful ruler, not only because she took the amulet, but because her power is greater than any others', encompassing all the colors of magic. But Kyrie wants to learn from her mother before taking it on. Show the empress among her people—she has not aged.

Show Eldric, who has aged, put their arm around Kyrie, who has not aged.

Appendix 2—250 Writing Prompts

1. A doctor who works in a busy city hospital takes a job in a small mountain town after losing one of their patients. They aren't running away, they just need some time to get over it, and they plan to return to the big city. The doctor regrets their decision soon after moving there but begins to like it over time. A big reason is the owner of the hardware store.

2. Write a book of subway stories—real events you've witnessed on the train.

3. Love is hard for empaths. When you can feel every emotion of another person, you lose track of what you, yourself, feel.

4. A couple who has been together for a very long time are flipping through the TV channels, while having a very deep conversation.

5. A group of teenagers decide to cut school and go hang out on the old water tower, only to find out that the water tower isn't what it seems to be.

6. A frustrated writer finds an old typewriter in an antique shop, and when they bring it home, they discover that they can write best-selling books with it.

7. An anthropologist discovers a cave in South America, where a small tribe of indigenous people have lived without any contact with modern civilization.

8. What was supposed to be a friend trip to a mountain cabin turns into a romantic weekend neither of them expected.

9. Is it better to give or receive?

10. A well-known artist loses the ability to create the kind of art they make, and they need to find another way to satisfy their unrelenting desire to create.

11. Write a story about needing to take a shower.

12. In your world, a young person must take a journey into the wilderness, and if they survive, they will become an adult. You have started your journey but are injured. An intriguing spirit saves your life, and you finish your journey, rewarded by being accepted into adulthood. Now, you must take a mate. Many come forward to win your hand, but one stands out, and you chose them. Right before the union ceremony, you discover they are the person who nursed you back from your injury. You were supposed to survive the journey on your own. Can you pretend it didn't happen? Or do you stop the union?

13. A woman is taking care of her mother, who has been diagnosed with a terminal illness, and the mother confesses to a terrible secret.

14. Write a story about checking into a hotel.

15. They declared theirs was a life-long friendship, but when one of them is called to take their rightful seat on the throne, and the other is called to fight in the Centurys War, that friendship is tested.

16. Write a version of *Snow White and the Seven Dwarves*, but each of the Dwarves is named after one of the seven deadly sins.

17. Write a story about surviving a blizzard.

18. Has there ever been a time when you did something you never thought you could?

19. A couple on their honeymoon at a secluded tropical resort is terrorized by another vacationer they meet at the pool bar.

20. A hiker, lost in the woods on a corporate retreat, stumbles into the campsite of a group of hippies. The hiker is grateful to be found, but the hippies are a little weird for them—except one. The hippie is still a hippie, but there's something about them that draws the hiker in. The hiker stays with the group for a few days, but when the hiker goes back to real life with the hippie, they both have to figure out if they can still be together.

21. If you could have a meal with anyone alive or dead, who would it be?

22. At three years old, they already knew they would be together forever.

23. A woman is pulled over for a traffic violation, but instead of getting a ticket, the officer takes one look at her and arrests her on the spot. When she gets to the station, there are three other women who look exactly like her, and each one of them is just as confused as she is.

24. You are a traveling salesman for an intergalactic paper company.

25. Your character is talking to their neighbor when the neighbor just sort of fades away right in front of them. When your character goes to the neighbor's wife to tell them what happened, the wife acts as if she never had a husband. This happens a few more times, and your character has to figure out what is going on.

26. Write a story about a falling out between two people that ends with one of them forgiving the other on their death bed.

27. They ran in different circles when they went to school together. Now that they're grown, they seem to have a lot more in common than they did back then. When it turns out that one of them is still friends with someone who bullied the other, things get hard.

28. They met and parted on an airplane flight, and both of their lives are changed.

29. The train's engineer has died, and none of the passengers knows until the train starts to dangerously speed up.

30. They keep meeting. One thinks it's fate. One doesn't believe in fate. Either way, they fall in love. Then something happens to separate them. The one who believes in fate loses hope. The one who doesn't believe in fate hopes with all their heart they're wrong.

31. The polar ice sheets have completely melted, and floating off-coast cities, once a part of the nearby countries they once belonged to, have declared themselves sovereign countries.

32. Write a story about a person who does unselfish things without letting anyone see them.

33. If you were a TikTok(er), what would you video?

34. A circle of friends become jealous of one of their own when it seems that she's discovered the fountain of youth.

35. On the first day of a new job, someone realizes they have been given a job they are not even remotely qualified to do.

36. A woman who has spent her life raising her kids, taking care of her parents, and being a perfect wife is suddenly freed from taking care of anyone when her parents pass away, her kids move out, and her husband leaves her for another man.

37. On a cold winter's evening, when a woman's car breaks down on the side of the road a few miles from home, a kind stranger offers her a warm pair of gloves and a ride home, which she gratefully accepts.

38. A person's boss is taking credit for their work.

39. An accident caused a woman to lose her sight. The person who caused it never officially met the woman but feels bad. They know the woman will never forgive them but do things to make the woman's life better out of guilt. A few years down the line, they meet at a party. The woman doesn't know the person she's talking to is the one who caused her blindness. They get along very well. Too well. Can the person who caused the accident confess to what they did?

40. A flower shop owner is obsessed with creating a new kind of rose.

41. A surf competition turns heated when a newcomer threatens to take the title from the revered repeat champion.

42. What does "healthy" mean, anyway?

43. Paintings in museums all over the world are being stolen, and no one seems to know how or who's doing it.

44. A farmer grows an unusual crop that everyone uses, but no one wants to know how the crop is grown.

45. A child who used to be afraid of the dark now controls the monsters they used to hide from.

46. If you had one superpower, what would it be? Write a story about a person with that power facing off with another superhero with the power to defeat them.

47. A man who has been babied and sheltered by his mother all his life finally has to take care of himself.

48. Write a story of a debate discussing which is better, cats or dogs, but from the perspective of both sides.

49. Your character is from a royal family, but it's very unlikely that they will get anywhere near the throne. So, they are left to their own devices, including choosing who they will marry, because it doesn't matter. They fall in love with a commoner, but just as they are to be married, a sequence of events makes your character the next in line to the throne. Now, the marriage is forbidden.

50. A group of kids on a camping trip find a circle of moss-covered stones in a shady glen. On one side of the circle grows an abundance of flowers. On the other, prickly brambles tangle among dead and bleached branches. When the kids step into the circle, the branches assemble to reveal a skeletal creature that demands they take sides in the war of the underworld.

51. A person lives in an apartment where they can hear everything going on in the living room above theirs through the heater vent.

52. In your character's world, love is only allowed for certain people, and your character isn't one of them. But your character meets someone and falls in love, even though it is forbidden. Now that they've experienced it, they want to love, even if it kills them.

53. Write about your deepest darkest secret.

54. Is there really love after divorce? Your character doesn't think so, until their high school sweetheart comes back into the picture, reigniting the love that has never really died for either of them. The problem is your character did something unforgivable to end the relationship in the first place. How can your character fix it?

55. A person lives in the countryside, with neighbors spread out far and wide. One day, a package arrives in the mail that was destined for a neighbor. Happy for the chance to meet their neighbor, they set out to deliver the package, but instead of being happy to receive it, the neighbor is angry and hostile. A few days later, the neighbor apologizes, and this begins a slow march toward romance.

56. A character receives one hundred million dollars and has to spend it all in one day. The catch is they have to spend it on themselves.

57. Your best friend is getting married to the wrong person, and you've been trying to tell her for months. Now, it's days before the wedding, and everyone is gathering at the island destination only to find out the reason you don't like the fiancée is because you are in love with her.

58. An inventor figures out how to put more time in a day, but there is a price to pay.

59. An engineer at a tech company is testing a new device that can predict people's health with various biometric monitors. However, they discover the device is smart enough to read the holder's mind. When they accidentally leave the device in a meeting room, one of their co-workers picks it up and hands it to them. When they realize what the co-worker is thinking, they are terrified.

60. A young woman inherits a hand mirror and finds she can talk to her dead grandmother through it.

61. Scientists find what's beyond the edge of the universe. What is it?

62. Go to your own social media page and find a post you made a long time ago. Write a story about the post as if it were written by someone else.

63. A couple is separated by war, and neither knows if the other is alive. Can they make it back to one another?

64. Take a scene from two of your favorite movies and combine them into one scene.

65. She's lived alone for years—or has she? Recently, she's noticed that the other side of the bed looks slept in. There are hairs on the pillow and in the basin that aren't hers. A glass that she didn't use is left in the sink. There's a sweater in her closet that isn't hers.

66. Write a story about just one day in the life of a stranger.

67. A teacher posts inspiring things she overhears her students saying around school and becomes a social media influencer. She becomes so obsessed with being a celebrity that she forgets who is supposed to be teaching who.

68. A family member has left you a box of jewelry.

69. Do you believe in ghosts? Write a ghost story from the perspective of a non-believer.

70. Write a story about someone who can't concentrate on an important task.

71. Someone wakes up from a long coma to find their spouse has moved on.

72. A wealthy eccentric befriends a person they see at a coffee shop every day.

73. Tired of the rat race, a businessperson decides to cash out their retirement and buy a bed and breakfast.

74. Write about a time you almost gave up.

75. Two people are staying at a hotel. One is there on business, and the other is there for an interview. A freak snowstorm shuts down the downtown area, postponing their appointments. The two people like each other, and things happen, even though both consider it a one-night stand. When they show up to their appointments, it turns out one is the other's hiring manager.

76. Write a story about a visit to a distant relative or old friend.

77. Write a story about the Grim Reaper coming to get you and you talking them out of it—for the time being.

78. Write a how-to book about an ordinary thing that you're really good at or, even better, that you're really bad at.

79. Suffering from depression and unable to get out of bed, a person makes friends with a lizard on their windowsill.

80. Write a story about a child losing their favorite toy.

81. They are brought together in an arranged marriage, but over time, they really fall in love.

82. Write a story that starts with someone being interviewed.

83. An alien civilization comes to Earth, and they are all female.

84. You've made some funny weather observations on your social media posts, and the local news station asks you to become their weather commentator.

85. The homeowner's association of a high-rise building requires prospective tenants to abide by unreasonable rules.

86. You're trapped in an elevator with your idol. How does it go?

87. The military is training an elite force of soldiers with telekinesis, and your character has just been recruited.

88. Wildfires threaten a wildlife park.

89. Prospects aren't great in your character's small town. Either they marry their childhood best friend or the manager of the shoe store who is the child of their mom's best friend, fresh back from college. Neither of them makes the character swoon. Then a new person comes to town and makes your character rethink everything they've ever known about themselves.

90. Someone discovers a magic stopwatch that can stop, rewind, and fast-forward time.

91. Several people get stuck on a subway car when the power goes out. Two of them absolutely rub each other the wrong way. Eventually, the power comes back on, and they go back to their lives, but for some reason they keep running into each other, even though it's a big city. At some point, they start to like each other, but neither will admit it, until something happens, and they fall in love.

92. Passengers in a single car of an amusement park ride are somehow sent down a track that is not normally part of the ride. Terror ensues.

93. A woman is walking down the street, minding her own business, when a stranger stops her and berates her for something in a very intelligent and convincing way. Why does the stranger stop her, and how does the woman react?

94. A blogger writes a 10-step plan for a happier life, picking random things, in a lazy attempt to get a blog post written for their once-a-week commitment. To their surprise, it goes viral, and they are invited on talk shows, Ted Talks, etc., to speak about their amazing list.

95. No one believes him when he tells them he has learned of a secret doorway to the in-between, which is frustrating because it requires a believing mind to enter.

96. A letter is written by someone who never intended to send it, but somehow, it gets sent.

97. A young girl, who doesn't get along with her mother, finds her mother's childhood diary and realizes they have more in common than she thought they did.

98. A poorly written memo is sent out to everyone in an office, with an urgent change to a frequently used process, but none of the recipients is brave enough to say they don't understand what it means. They each try to comply with their own interpretation of what they think it means.

99. The ten-year-old child of a man wrongly convicted of a crime tries to find a way to prove his dad is innocent.

100. The story ends with everyone unconscious but the dog.

101. You have been aware that there are parallel realities since you were a child, but no one believed you; even worse, some believed you were mentally ill because of it. You learned to hide it.

102. Open the book closest to you and write a story about the first sentence on the first page.

103. Based on records found deep beneath the pyramids, it turns out that Earth was initially populated by a distant civilization that discovered the gene for a predisposition for criminality and lack of empathy, and everyone with the gene was culled and relocated to Earth. Now we know where our ancestors are and how to get back.

104. Write a real current news event into your story as a part of the setting.

105. Write about a dream you've had.

106. His wife works at a travel agency, which means they get to go on a lot of great trips. On one of these trips, he puts together that his wife isn't a travel agent at all but a hired assassin, and on each of the trips they've gone on someone very prominent has died.

107. Your hometown paper prints an impossible puzzle each day, and people win prizes for solving it first. But the current puzzle has been running for a very long time because no one can solve it. You are eating breakfast one day, and the answer comes to you.

108. The story includes a person walking an odd array of animals.

109. He and his wife argue all the time about his love of sports hunting. She won't let him display his trophies at home, so his office at work has to do. It's gotten so bad that they're on the brink of divorce. That's why he's surprised when she gives him a hunting trip for his birthday. It changes everything for him, and he thinks their marriage is saved—until he shows up at the hunting lodge, his wife is there, and he finds out that he will be the hunted, not the hunter.

110. A person meets and spends time with someone they instantly connect with, but they are separated before they exchange names or contact info. The only thing they can use to identify the person is a scent.

111. What was the last nice thing a stranger did for you? Tell the story from their perspective.

112. Take your favorite quote and incorporate it into your story.

113. Your character's spouse starts coming home with injuries they won't talk about. Your character follows them one day and finds the spouse has lost their job, has been competing in an illegal fighting ring for the prize money, but now can't get out.

114. A big-city woman inherits her grandparents' farm.

115. Everyone thinks the sweet old woman who is the current queen is mostly a figurehead. They couldn't be more wrong.

116. A group of friends, who always joked about building a commune because they get along so well, actually decide to do it.

117. What is the meaning of this exact moment? How will it affect the rest of your life?

118. Two best friends win a shopping spree at a local grocery store.

119. She gets a job at the used bookstore and is amazed by what happens after the store closes each night.

120. What illustration did you see in your childhood and still remember today? How did it make you feel? Do you think the artist intended for you to feel that way?

121. Write a story about kindergarteners telling each other jokes.

122. You think you're losing your mind because you see things happening that no one else does. One day you realize you are seeing into another dimension, and as soon as you realize it, you can control it. It gives you amazing powers.

123. A superstitious person sees the same symbol everywhere and starts to get very paranoid.

124. Your aunt has always been slightly off her rocker, and most of the family has kind of turned their back on her except you. Sure, she sometimes makes you roll your eyes, but you don't think she's that bad. But now she's become infirm and terrified of living in a home. You're the only one she will live with.

125. A person who has never ridden a bike before makes a plan to bike across the US.

126. You get an unexpected free day off, after not having had a day off in longer than you can remember. There are so many things you've wanted to do, and thankfully you've been keeping a list.

127. Write a story with twenty-six characters, and each one's name starts with a different letter of the alphabet.

128. A story about unlikely superheroes with weird powers.

129. Write a story about someone who has always had their eye on something they see as the ultimate prize, but the closer they get to it, the more they realize the price to get there is too high.

130. Something you post on social media becomes a frequently shared quote.

131. A street racing club disrupts the lives of a quiet town.

132. A scientist studying octopuses and how they regrow lost limbs, discovers that they are not originally from Earth. The discovery triggers a military response, and the octopuses are forced to reveal their true reason for colonizing the deepest reaches of Earth's oceans.

133. What was the biggest risk you ever took? Write a story about it.

134. Mysterious seeds arrive in the mail, and a gardener plants them in their backyard. What they grow astounds them.

135. The man is grown now, but his imaginary friend is still very much part of his life.

136. A woman has the same dream every night, only it gets longer, revealing more of the dream each night. In the dream, time is going backward until she realizes she's watching a murder, from end to start. Soon, she begins to believe it really happened.

137. Dating a best friend's ex is never a good idea—even if they say it's okay. Because they're lying. Don't trust them, even if you really, really want to. Nothing good will ever come from it if you do. But you do it anyway. Whose heart ends up broken?

138. You gave a movie a bad review, and it went viral. Now the whole cast is trying get you to change your mind.

139. A fourth grader tries to earn enough money for a pair of shoes that are advertised to make them play a sport really well.

140. A social media influencer, who specializes in beauty products, discovers that the proprietary ingredient in a popular anti-aging serum comes from the brainstem of infants that only works on the biological mother. At the same time, a string of celebrity pregnancy rumors turns out to be untrue—but are they?

141. A personality for a popular podcast about relationships is adamant that there is no such thing as fate. One of her listeners doesn't agree and wants to make her believe. So, they go on a mission to run into the podcaster as often as they can in an effort to establish a friendship and ultimately get the podcaster to admit to fate being the reason they kept on meeting. It's manipulative, the listener knows, but they think the podcaster is manipulative in shaming people for believing in fate, so it all equals out. The listener doesn't plan on falling in love, though.

142. Write an adventure story that takes place without ever leaving a house.

143. How did someone die in your favorite dive bar?

144. A family goes on a picnic in the park. Everything seems casual on the surface, but the family is dealing with something huge they aren't talking about.

145. You journey to a foreign country for work and decide to break the company rules and travel beyond the area you are authorized to go. Everything you own is stolen, including your phone and ID. What do you do?

146. A complex murder mystery that starts with a child losing their favorite blanket on an airplane.

147. A kid falls asleep on the bus on the way home from school. The bus driver doesn't notice and parks the bus in the bus yard, leaving the child to figure out how to get home on their own.

148. Write a holiday story.

149. A group of kids play Clue and get it into their heads they need to figure out who killed the woman down the street, even though everyone has been told it was an accident.

150. Write a story about you based entirely from your mailperson's perspective.

151. Rummage through your junk drawer and select five random items. Work them into your story.

152. A person is having a conversation with someone who is unable to speak or move, only communicate by the look in their eyes.

153. What kind of movie do you like? If you had to write about your day as if it were a scene in one of those movies, how would it go?

154. A cynical person gets an astrological reading, and what they hear convinces them that the reading was accurate.

155. Tell the story of a person who travels the world looking for interesting meals.

156. Write a story using as many clichés as you can.

157. An art restorer at a museum finds the wig on a sculpture comes off, and a treasure is inside the sculpture's head.

158. A scientist discovers a doorway to the place where the souls of dead people live.

159. A worker at an AI company finds out that their coworkers have been being replaced by human-robot hybrids.

160. Write a story about a place you would like to go to when you need peace in your life.

161. Write a story about a writer of rhyming verse, who has lost the ability to rhyme.

162. A peaceful society maintains universal balance. They perform their task without question. Their efforts only work because their world is ancient and has remained unchanged for several millennia, having been contained within a protective orb. An intruder enters the orb and introduces the society to modern ideals, threatening the society and all it protects.

163. Tell one of your childhood memories from someone else's perspective.

164. Write a story about the power of fire, water, wind, earth, air, or all of them.

165. Having grown up in a rural town, the winner of a national talent competition finds it difficult to deal with their success.

166. A woman has been told all her life that it's more important for her make others happy than it is to make herself happy. This has caused her to pay more attention to others, and she's lost sight of who she really is. Now she's grown, and her life feels out of balance because she hasn't spent enough time trying to figure out what makes her happy.

167. Some people are afraid that robots will take over the world. Write a story about your thoughts on the subject.

168. A song changed her life.

169. A birthday party that goes perfectly to plan, but the guest of honor is not happy.

170. The oldest person in the world is celebrating their birthday on live television and reveals the secret to their longevity.

171. Dinosaurs did not go extinct; they were gathered up and relocated to another planet. The beings who did this are back to do the same to the current animals, including humans.

172. An attitude of gratitude program in a middle school teaches kids that they have no idea about other kids' lives.

173. How do you start your day most mornings? Write a story about everything going wrong.

174. Two people meet and have the same amounts of attraction and repulsion for one another. They decide it isn't worth it but can't stay away from one another.

175. Do you have a nickname? How did you get it?

176. A well-known YouTube gamer tests out a new virtual reality game during his latest episode and disappears into the game in front of his entire audience. The world watches as he tries to get out.

177. Do you wish you had a nickname? What would it be?

178. Signs are popping up all over town saying good things about each of the residents.

179. A person finds a stack of receipts that tell an entire story about a week in someone's life.

180. A person's life is not going as planned, and everything seems to be falling apart, until someone claiming to be their fairy godmother shows up, at which point things go from bad to worse. It turns out the fairy godmother isn't very good at her job and is actually on probation. Can the two of them help each other?

181. Most people have had an interesting experience with customer support. Write a humorous story based on an experience you've had.

182. A person experiences random amounts of time as a future version of themselves.

183. The world is a different place after a freak magnetic storm sweeps the galaxy, ruining all electronic devices on Earth. Most of the population has died off from the resulting famines, wars, diseases, and lack of clean water. The remaining people have moved to protected cities on the coasts and the land between has become wild again. Your character is a wanderer who travels the in-between.

184. Each morning, a teacher arrives in their classroom to find a new note written on the dry erase board.

185. During renovations on an apartment building that used to be a famous hotel, a contractor finds letters and other mementos from a much earlier time period tucked inside the walls.

186. Write a story about someone trying to find someone in a crowd.

187. After a perfect first date, what's the appropriate time frame to wait to call someone to ask them out again? Write a story about a series of missed calls, texts, and emails that two people send to each other, maneuvering for a second date, while trying not to be too eager. The funny thing is they both really like each other.

188. A group of marijuana farmers are so off the grid that they don't know that marijuana has been legalized. They continue to sell to people as if it is a very risky thing, and the customers think the "old time drug deal experience" is just a marketing gimmick.

189. A romance that takes place on a farm.

190. After signing up on a dating web site, your character starts to suspect that some of the people aren't there for dating because some people in the profiles are ending up dead.

191. A person who has two families that don't know about each other.

192. You participate in a competitive audition to be in a commercial for a local business.

193. A boss decides to do an off-site meeting for all their employees at a corporate cohesiveness camp, and trust exercises and team building events go completely off the rails.

194. The secret to time travel is found in what makes rainbows.

195. She discovered the path to world peace, and she regrets it. It doesn't take long to get peace to spread. It turns out that people are inherently kind, and now that the path is clear, the natural condition of civilization is absolute peace. But you know what peace is in addition to natural? Boring. Now the world is bored, unhappy, and lazy. Now world leaders have to work for moments of discord just to make people happy and productive again.

196. Write the sappiest love story you can think of.

197. The neighbor across the street is doing something in their backyard. Truckloads upon truckloads of dirt are hauled away, and frankly, you're a little annoyed that it goes on day and night. You're down in the basement doing laundry one day, when your basement wall falls in and your neighbor is standing there. "We need to get you out of here," they say, gesturing impatiently.

198. Write the most unlikely romance you can think of.

199. Friends on a trip to New Orleans find a doll hidden behind a brick they accidentally knock out of place on one of the historic buildings in the French Quarter.

200. Bored out of his mind at his job as an administrative assistant for the government, a non-descript guy randomly punches buttons in the elevator. Somehow, the combination takes him deep beneath the building into a secret high-tech facility.

201. In a family with three grown children, each child has a vastly different memory of their childhood.

202. Write a story about a five-minute period in a very busy place, such as an airport, a busy street corner, a classroom, etc.

203. Write a character in your story who is exactly like you.

204. You have transformed into a dog.

205. A writer finds a magic pen that takes his mundane story ideas and makes them amazing. One day it runs out of ink.

206. Three people come to the same obstacle (a wall, a decision, a fork in the road, etc.) and each addresses it in a different way, but each has the exact same outcome.

207. Write a story that uses food to progress the plot from beginning to end.

208. Kids are going missing all over town, and the only common interaction they have is with the school lunch lady.

209. Test driving a prototype automobile, the driver discovers the vehicle does way more than the tech company who created it has divulged.

210. A door-to-door salesman peddles happiness.

211. He was the biggest nerd at his school before he left for college, but he's now a successful ad executive. She was too cool for school, and half the student body was terrified of her, including him, whom she used to tease unmercifully. Little did anyone know she had a good reason for acting so tough. Now, they're working for the same company, and they've been assigned to the same project. They pretend not to know each other. But he has resentment, and she has guilt. After completing a difficult assignment, things happen between them, and the distance they've maintained is forgotten. What happens next?

212. In the future, the coasts of a continent are the only habitable place to live. One coast is peaceful and beautiful, while the other is over-populated and overrun with crime. A lottery allows people from the overrun coast to move to the other coast, and the prize is a fast car. The contestants have to survive the long drive to win.

213. What was your happiest moment? Write a fictionalized story about it happening to the unlikeliest of people.

214. There are countless stories about non-human things being anthropomorphized. But is there a way to de-anthropomorphize a human? Write that story.

215. A dozen volunteers for a cryobank, who were frozen as test subjects one hundred years earlier, are taken out of deep freeze.

216. Write a story that incorporates the last text you sent.

217. Your character finds out that their spouse has been videoing their every move.

218. Pressured to join an online dating site by their friends, your character fills out their profile with information just the opposite of what they like. That way, they can say the site didn't work for them. But it turns out that they meet the person of their dreams.

219. After a terrible bicycling accident, a woman wakes up from her injuries in the hospital to find she has received a donated limb that seems to have a mind of its own.

220. Strange white vans with darkened windows are roaming through a large city, and a group of kids want to get to the bottom of things.

221. There used to be a place in Nevada called The Chicken Ranch. Your character used to work there.

222. Write a story about someone in solitary confinement.

223. Hollywood's most eligible bachelor is notoriously picky. Women throw themselves at him, but he couldn't care less. Until he meets his new costar, who won't give him the time of day. He keeps trying, though, and he becomes the most pathetic person around as he lavishes her with attention, while she just gets more and more aloof. There's a reason for her behavior, though.

224. In a world of terrible unhappiness, each person is given one day of absolute joy.

225. When a fire alarm goes off and the aquarium facility is evacuated, a performer who plays a mermaid is forgotten inside a sealed underwater tank overnight. To make things worse, the sealed chamber, which is partitioned off during the day, is opened to predatory fish during the night.

226. Have you ever shared something with someone, only to regret it?

227. In a kingdom far, far away, the gardens each resident grows reflect what's inside their hearts.

228. Your character finds a phone on the bus. They are about to turn it into the driver when the phone rings and the caller ID displays the character's name and picture.

229. They meet for the first time while working at a car wash. They meet for the second time at a ballet performance. They meet for a third and final time at the funeral of a mutual friend. Each time they meet, they fall in love.

230. Throughout her life, a young woman has occasionally caught glimpses of someone who appears to be watching her. But the glimpses are only that, brief sightings, and then they're gone. She used to think they were in her imagination or some sort of optical trick. But now that this is happening more often, she suspects the person watching her is herself.

231. Not everything is hard to do. Write a fictionalized story about something that some people find difficult to do but which you find super easy.

232. People who voluntarily agreed to have an identification chip implanted in them in an old study are now hearing voices telling them to do dangerous things.

233. Students at rival colleges sneak around to date each other because the penalty of dating someone from the other college is death.

234. Make music a primary topic within your story.

235. A feral cat in a quiet community helps a retired resident fight crime by leading them to evidence needed to solve the crimes.

236. Four people who don't know each other are dealing with issues in their own lives, but they have the local recreation center in common.

237. Pick a decade in the 1900s and make that the time period of your story.

238. Describe how it feels to have a glass of water upon stumbling out of the desert after being lost for a couple of days.

239. Write a war story, only it features kids on a playground.

240. One morning when the sun comes up, all the buildings in downtown are covered with webs, and egg sacs dangle among them. As the sun shines through them, human-like shapes are visible moving inside them.

241. You hurt someone by accident many years ago and never forgot it. You're given a chance to go back in time and redo the thing that hurt them. With one catch. It means they'd have a completely different life. They would not be aware that their life has changed, but they would feel a mourning for the loss of the life they would have lived.

242. A kid moves from the country to the big city and has to learn how to blend in with the kids at their new school.

243. How do you help someone else find hope in a hopeless situation?

244. Years earlier, your character's spouse disappeared. Now they're back and acting like they were never gone.

245. Write about a time when you found out the truth about something you'd been led to believe was completely different.

246. Thirty years after high school graduation, the class of 1985 is being murdered one by one. Who is doing it and why?

247. A story about the same person walking the same path on three different days, with three different experiences.

248. Fictionalize a well-known historic event.

249. There is a world where robots created humans, and the robots are worried that humans, with their ability to accept illogical things, will surpass them in intellect and take over the world.

250. The story ends with a heavy sigh.

Appendix 3—Planning Worksheets

myinkslinger

Target Audience Worksheet

- What kind of story, or genre, are you writing? (Genres often come with a specific audience already identified)
- Why are you writing this particular story?
- What message do you want your story to impart?
- Is there a specific audience who the message will best suit?

Demographics

Category	Target Audience
Age	
Location	
Gender	
Income	
Education	
Marital or Family Status	
Occupation	
Ethnic Background	

Notes

myinkslinger

Genre Worksheet

Sometimes writers know exactly what kind of books or stories they want to write. Other times, they have a hard time pinning their preferred genre down. And sometimes, a story can contain elements of multiple genres. An example of this might be a story about the civil war that also contains romance. Or a story about young people fighting against a corrupt government in the future. The genre of your book will fall within the category that is most prominent in the story. If it feels like there is an even amount of time dedicated to one element or another, you get to pick which one you like, and the others can be assigned as sub-genres.

To see a list of writing genres visit: https://en.wikipedia.org/wiki/List_of_writing_genres

What kind of books do you like to read?

Refer to the genre guide (see link above) and find the genre that best fits your answer:

Are there things you don't want to read or write about?

Refer to the genre guide (see link above) and find the genre that best fits your answer:

Are there certain tropes (cliches) you're drawn to or don't care for?

Refer to the genre guide (see link above) and find the genre that best fits your answer:

Is there a specific message you want to get across?

Refer to the genre guide (see link above) and find the genre that best fits your answer:

What audience do I want to reach?

Refer to the genre guide (see link above) and find the genre that best fits your answer:

Are there certain settings you like to write about?

Refer to the genre guide (see link above) and find the genre that best fits your answer:

What conflicts in stories do you like to write about?

Refer to the genre guide (see link above) and find the genre that best fits your answer:

What other details about genre do you find appealing?

Refer to the genre guide (see link above) and find the genre that best fits your answer:

What genre(s) appears most frequently here?

Despite the findings on this form, is there a genre that stands out to you? That is likely the genre you should write in.

inkstacks.com/inkslinger/genre

Story Arc Worksheet

Theme:

Climax:

The Story Arc

Exposition: Introduces the main character(s) to the reader, tells what problem is to be solved, and sets the place and tone. Main character(s) and problem to be solved, inciting incident, setting time, setting place.

9. _____

8. _____

7. _____

6. _____

5. _____

4. _____

3. _____

2. _____

1. _____

Major Plot Points

Falling Action

Rising Action

10. _____

11. _____

12. _____

13. _____

14. _____

Resolution:

Rising Action: The build up of tension to the climax explaining what the story is about and contains the inciting incident.

Climax: This is the main character(s)' moment of truth.

Falling Action: Describes the consequences to the actions of the character(s), tying up loose ends.

Exposition:

Resolution: How the story ends, closing the loop of the story.

inkstacks.com/inkslinger/story-arc

myinkslinger

Point of View (POV) Worksheet

Determining What Point of View (POV) to Use in Your Story:

Select the description that makes the most sense for your story in respect to each of the following five questions.

Use additional note pages at end for any notes you would like to take.

1. **How much distance do you want to put between the reader and the narrator?**

   A. You want the reader to feel like they are in the mind of the characters

   B. You want the reader to feel like they are literally a character in the story.

   C. You want to leave a certain amount of distance between the narrator and the reader.

2. **How much information do you need to convey to the reader throughout the story?**

   A. You want the reader to know everything happening in this story.

   B. You need to instruct the reader on how to do things.

   C. You want to keep a sense of mystery about one or more aspects of the story.

3. **How reliable do you want the narrator to be?**

   A. It is most important that the reader feel a connection to the character, even if the character is flawed.

   B. The narrator needs to talk directly to the reader.

   C. You want the reader to rely on the narrator as a trusted source of all aspects of the story.

4. **What kind and how much information do you need to provide to the reader?**

   A. One or more characters have information that needs to be conveyed to the reader without letting other characters know.

   B. The book is a step-by-step instruction on how to do something.

   C. You nee to reveal a surprise climax or ending that none of the characters see coming.

5. **How important is developing a connection between the reader and the characters?**

   A. There is a specific character you want the reader to connect with.

   B. You want the reader to be the direct focus of the narrator.

   C. You want the reader to connect to several characters.

What your selections mean: if you picked mostly:

   A. You probably want to write your story with a First Person point of view.

   B. You are probably writing a How To book and Second Person will be an effective point of view.

   C. Third Person point of view will probably be your preferred point of view.

Keep in mind, these are just suggestions. Only you know the best point of view in which to tell your story. Authors are creative and like to bend the "rules" so if that's you, do your thing and have fun!

When in doubt, Third Person point of view is effective in almost all kinds of stories

my**inkslinger**

Outline Worksheet

Beat Sheet

Story Title:

Story Blurb:

Beats	Detail	Chapter(s)
Act One	**Reader hook introduces characters, exposition, set up major conflict**	
Inciting Incident	What starts the characters on their journey?	
Begin the Rising Action	What events force the characters forward?	
Act Two	**What conflicts occur to force the characters forward?**	
Minor conflict #1	Increase the tension with additional conflict.	
Midpoint	Explain why the character(s) must go forward.	
Minor conflict #2	Increase the tension with additional conflict.	
Crisis	What makes the characters doubt they will succeed?	
Act Three	**The main character(s) overcomes hurdles to succeed**	
Climax	What is the turning point in the story?	
Resolution	What did the character(s) learn or how did they change?	

Notes

my**inkslinger**

Setting Worksheet

Story Title:

Story Blurb:

Where does the
story take place?
List the settings
with a short
description:

When does the
story take place?
List the times/
periods:

What are the
moods of the
settings?

myinkslinger

Character Sketch Worksheet

Story Title:

Story Blurb:

Character Name:

Physical Description:

Character Traits:

What is their motivation (desires)?

What do they fear?

Where do they live?

Who are their friends, family, pets?

myinkslinger

Conflict Worksheet

Story Title:

Character:

Internal Conflict: A character has conflict within themselves.

Internal Conflict:

Actions/
reactions:

External Conflict: The conflict is outside of the character's control.

External Conflict:

Actions/
reactions:

Appendix 4—Cited works

The following works have been cited in this book as either examples or reference material and the authors wish to thank the authors for their contribution to the art of writing and to the crafting of *Inkslinger 2—Planning Your Amazing Book*.

All works are listed below in alphabetical order by title.

Books

All the Light We Cannot See by Anthony Doerr, Scribner, 2014

American Psycho by Bret Eastern, Vintage, 1991

The Art of Character: Creating Memorable Characters for Fiction, Films, and TV by David Corbett, Penguin Books, 2013

Beowulf, author unknown, oldest written form is a single written medieval manuscript, likely originally composed between 700 and 750

The Book Thief, by Markus Zusak, Picador, 2005

Carrie by Stephen King, Anchor Books, 1st edition 2011

The Chronicles of Narnia, by C.S. Lewis, Geoffrey Bles, 1950

The Curious Incident of the Dog in the Night-Time by Mark Haddon, Doubleday, 2003

Dead Souls by Nikolai Gogol, publisher unknown, 1842

Discworld, series of 41 novels by Terry Pratchett, Transworld Publishers Doubleday Random House, 1983

Divergent by Veronica Roth, Harper Collins, 2011

Eugene Onegin: A Novel in Verse by Alexander Pushkin, published in serial form by an unknown Russian press between 1825 and 1832

Fight Club by Chuck Palahniuk, W. W. Norton, 1996

Forrest Gump by Winston Groom, Doubleday, 1986

A Game of Thrones by George R. R. Martin, Bantam Spectra, 1996

The Girl on the Train, by Paula Hawkins, Penguin Publishing Group, 2015

Half-Asleep in Frog Pajamas by Tom Robbins, Bantam Books, 1994

Harry Potter and the Sorcerer's Stone by J.K. Rowling, Scholastic Press, 1997

Hills Like White Elephants by Ernest Hemingway, originally published in the literary magazine transition (sic), 1927

The Hours by Michael Cunningham, Farrar, Straus and Giroux, 1998

Huckleberry Finn by Mark Twain, originally published by Charles L. Webster and Company, 1884

The Hunger Games by Suzanne Collins, Scholastic, 2008

Inkslinger—99-Day Guided Writing Experience by Kimberly Cooper Griffin, Night River Press, 2020

Into the Wild by Jon Krakaur, Anchor Books; 1st edition, 1997

It by Stephen King, Viking, 1986

It Was an Affair by Finnian Burnett in the anthology *Conference Call*, edited by Ann Roberts, Bella Books, 2007

Kindred by Octavia Butler, Beacon Press, 1979

The Lord of the Rings Trilogy by J.R.R. Tolkien, originally published by Allen & Unwin, 1954

The Martian Chronicles by Ray Bradbury, Doubleday, 1950

The Metamorphosis by Franz Kafka, originally published by Kurt Wolff Verlag, 1915

Never Let Me Go by Kazuo Ishiguro, Vintage International, 2005

Nightmares in the Sky: Gargoyles and Grotesques by Stephen King, Viking Studio Books, 1988

Point of View: How to use the different POV types, avoid head-hopping, and choose the best point of view for your book (Writers' Guide Series) by Sandra Gerth, Ylva Publishing, 2016

Pride and Prejudice by Jane Austen, originally published by T. Egerton, Whitehall, 1813

Pride and Prejudice and Zombies by Jane Austin and Seth Grahame-Smith, Titan Books, 2016

The Princess Bride by William Goldman, Harcourt Brace Jovanovich, 1973

Romancing the Beat: Story Structure for Romance Novels by Gwen Hayes, Gwen Hayes, 2016

Romeo and Juliet by William Shakespeare, originally published by Cuthbert Burby, 1599

A Rose for Emily by William Faulkner, originally published in *The Forum Magazine*, 1930

Save the Cat! The Last Book on Screenwriting You'll Ever Need by Blake Snyder, Michael Wiese Productions, 2005

Song of Solomon by Toni Morrison, Alfred Knopf, 1977

Star Wars by Alan Dean Foster (Credited to George Lucas), Ballantine, 1976

Stardust by Neil Gaiman, DC Comics, 1999

Station Eleven by Emily St. John Mandel Knopf Doubleday Publishing Group, 2014

Structuring Your Novel: Essential Keys for Writing an Outstanding Story by K.M. Weiland PenForASword Publishing, 2013

Their Eyes Were Watching God by Zora Neale Hurston, J. B. Lippincott, 1937

Tom Sawyer by Mark Twain, originally published by American Publishing Company, June 1876

The Weird Sisters by Eleanor Brown, Amy Einhorn Books/Putnam, 2011

What Dreams May Come by Richard Matheson, G. P. Putnam's Sons, 1978

The Wizard of Oz by L. Frank Baum, George M. Hill Company, 1900

Write Characters Your Readers Won't Forget (Toolkits for Emerging Writers Book 1) by Stant Litore, Westmarch Publishing, 2015

Films

Alien, screenplay by Dan O'Bannon and Ronald Shusett, distributed by 20th Century Fox, directed by Ridley Scott, produced by Gordon Carroll, David Giler and Walter Hill, 1979

Big Chill, The, screenplay by Lawrence Kasden and Barbara Benedek, distributed by Columbia Pictures, directed by Lawrence Kasden, produced by Michael Shamberg, 1983

Black Panther, screenplay by Ryan Coogler and Joe Robert Cole, based on the comic books by Stan Lee and Jack Kirby, distributed by Walt Disney Studios Motion Pictures, directed by Ryan Coogler, Produced by Kevin Feige, 2018

Bridesmaids, screenplay by Kristen Wiig and Annie Mumolo, distributed by

Universal Pictures, directed by Paul Feig, produced by Judd Aptow, Barry Mendel and Clayton Townsend, 2011

Castaway, screenplay by William Broyles Jr., distributed by 20th Century Fox, directed and produced by Robert Zemeckis, 2000

The Holiday, screenplay by Nancy Meyers, distributed by Sony Pictures Releasing, directed by Nancy Meyers, Produced by Nancy Meyers and Bruce A. Block, 2006

An Officer and a Gentleman, screenplay by Douglas Day Stewart, distributed by Paramount Pictures, directed by Taylor Hackford, produced by Martin Elfand and Douglas Day Stewart, 1982

The Photograph screenplay by Stella Meghie, distributed by Universal Pictures, directed by Stella Maghie, Produced by James Lopez and Will Packer, 2020

Pretty Woman, screenplay by J. F. Lawton, distributed by Buena Vista Pictures, directed by Garry Marshall, produced by Arnon Milchan, Steven Reuthar and Gary W. Goldstein, 1990

The Sixth Sense, screenplay by M. Night Shyamalan, distributed by Buena Vista Pictures Distribution, directed by M. Night Shyamalan, produced by Frank Marshall, Kathleen Kennedy and Barry Mendel, 1999

Sleepless in Seattle, screenplay by Nora Ephron, Jeff Arch and David S. Ward, distributed by TriStar Pictures, directed by Nora Ephron, produced by Gary Foster, 1993

Stand by Me, screenplay by Bruce A. Evans and Raynold Gideon, distributed by Columbia Pictures, directed by Rob Reiner, produced by Act III Pictures, 1986, based on the novella *The Body* by Stephen King, published by Viking, 1982

The Usual Suspects, screenplay by Christopher McQuarrie, distributed by Gramercy Pictures, directed by Bryan Singer, produced by Bryan Singer and Michael McDonnell, 1995

About the Authors

Finnian Burnett teaches undergrad English and creative writing. They also run an online writing academy for a non-profit organization and will corner people at parties to talk about the thrill of finding the perfect story structure. Finn believes anyone can become a great writer if they're willing to read, write, and accept critical feedback.

Under their former name, Finn published several books with Sapphire Books publishing, including two Rainbow Award Winners. A self-published book, Coyote Ate the Stars, won first place in fantasy in the Writer's Digest Self-Published Book Awards.

Finn is enamored with flash fiction and leads classes and workshops on the structure of a flash story. They've published in the Daily Science Fiction, Flash Fiction Magazine, the Bath Flash Fiction Festival anthology, Black Hare Press, and more. They are currently working on a flash-in-novella project and a queer Shakespeare retelling.

In their spare time, Finn secretly crushes on Constable George Crabtree from the Murdoch Mysteries, watches a lot of Star Trek, and takes their cat, Lord Gordo, for walks in a stroller. Finn lives in British Columbia with their wife and Lord Gordo.

Finn can be found at www.finnburnett.com and on Twitter under @FinnianBurnett

Kimberly Cooper Griffin is an award-winning author and a software designer. Her technical career spans almost three decades and while she's always been a writer, she's focused on it more recently, effectively melding her technical and creative passions. Over that time, she has pondered two major issues:

1 - Publishing has a diversity problem

2 - The overly complex process of getting published, whether through self-publishing or a traditional publisher

She attributes these issues to the barriers to entry: time, money, and knowledge. These have led to marginalized voices getting left behind in an historically straight, white, cis male-dominated industry.

To address this, with the help of partners, she founded a software company called Inkstacks, which is working to establish a nurturing community for writers that provides software-guided navigation, simplifying a complicated process to produce high-quality manuscripts. This supports all writers, particularly marginalized groups who have been historically shut out of a clear path toward publication.

Kimberly's vision is to provide writers with visibility and readers and publishers with a wider, richer pool of diverse talent, by removing hurdles, and allowing writers to do what they love to do most—write.

Kimberly can be found at www.KimberlyCooperGriffin.com and on Twitter @kcoopergriffin.